REFLECTIONS ON OUR CHRISTIAN FAITH AND LIFE

REFLECTIONS ON OUR CHRISTIAN FAITH AND LIFE

by

Bishop Gerasimos Papadopoulos

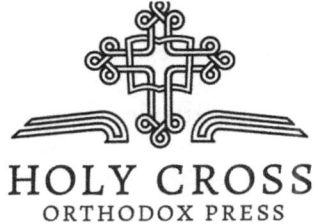

HOLY CROSS
ORTHODOX PRESS

Brookline, Massachusetts

© Holy Cross Orthodox Press, 1995
Reprint 2023
Published by Holy Cross Orthodox Press
Hellenic College, Inc.
50 Goddard Avenue
Brookline, MA 02445

All rights reserved. No part of this publication may be reproduced, stored in a retrieval system, or transmitted in any form or by any means—electronic, mechanical, photocopy, recording, or other—without the prior written permission of the publisher.

ISBN 978-1-885652-37-9
ISBN 1-885632-12-7

Cover Design by Nicholas J. Botsolis

Library of Congress Cataloging-inPublication Data

Names: Papadopoulos, Gerasimos, author.
Title: Reflections on our Christian faith and life / by Bishop Gerasimos Papadopoulos.
Description: Reprint edition. | Brookline, Massachusetts : Holy Cross Orthodox Press, [2023] | First published by Holy Cross Orthodox Press in 1995.
Identifiers: ISBN: 978-1-885652-37-9
Subjects: LCSH: Meditations. | Faith--Meditations. | Faith and reason--Orthodox Eastern Church--Meditations. | Christian life--Meditations. | Spiritual life--Orthodox Eastern Church--Meditations. | Spirituality--Orthodox Eastern Church--Meditations. | Salvation--Orthodox Eastern Church--Meditations. | Jesus Christ--Passion--Meditations. | Holiness--Orthodox Eastern Church--Meditations. | Trinity--Meditations.

Classification: LCC: BV4811|b.P317 2023 | DDC: 248.4/819--dc23

CONTENTS

PREFACE	9
PROLOGUE	11

A. INTRODUCTORY REFLECTIONS

1. The Spirituality of Man	15
2. The Revelation of God	18
3. Faith and Knowledge	20
4. Faith and the Church	21

B. THE MYSTERY OF THE DIVINE PLAN OF SALVATION IN CHRIST

1. A Hidden Mystery	24
2. The Person and the Work of Christ	27
3. "Who Do Men Say That I Am?" (Mk. 8:27).	28
4. The Mystery of the Holy Trinity	33

5. The Relationship of the Son and the Holy Spirit	45
6. The Incarnation	49

C. OUR SALVATION THROUGH THE PASSION OF CHRIST

1. The Cross of Christ	57
2. Our Salvation in Christ	66
3. Christ and the Church (Col. 1:18-23)	78
4. Sin and the Divine Plan of Salvation	87
5. The Resurrection, the Ascension	92
6. The Divine Plan of Salvation in the History of the World	103

D. OUR CHRISTIAN LIFE

1. Divine Grace and the Gifts of the Holy Spirit	121
2. The Fruit of the Holy Spirit (Gal. 5:22)	130
3. The Armor of God	161
4. The Church in its Spiritual Struggle	173

E. THE HOLINESS OF MAN

1. Introduction	185
2. Holiness in Christ	187
3. In the Holy Spirit	188
4. Synergy, Personal Struggle	189

5. Stages in the Spiritual Ascent	190
6. The Journey Toward Holiness	194
7. Man is Between Heaven and Earth	202
8. Conclusion	204

F. CONCLUDING QUESTIONS AND REFLECTIONS

1. The Christian Faith as Religious Experience of Redemption	209
2. Perennial Questions of Christian Faith	212
3. What in Reality Does Christ Ask of Us?	217
4. The Hope of the Resurrection of the Dead	221
5. Negative Questions	224
6. The Name of God and the New Ideas of Each Age	225
7. Religion, Faith, Mind, and Heart	237

PREFACE

His Grace, Bishop Gerasimos of Abydos is a pastor who cares about the members of the Christian flock, who listens to their questions, who understands how their concerns arise, and who responds, speaking to their hearts and minds with his own heart and mind as a compassionate and generous father.

In this book, Reflections On Our Christian Faith & Life, he reflects on the classical Christian themes and addresses numerous concerns expressed by the members of the Church. The reader will notice immediately the spiritual interests of the author in the articulation of the traditional themes, and the gentle presence of a genuine spiritual father seeking to guide and edify his spiritual children in the Christian life.

In the Reflections of Bishop Gerasimos, the reader feels the presence of this blessed man as he draws on the Orthodox Christian tradition and his own spiritual experience to articulate basic themes of Christian faith and life. Central to his presentation of these reflections is the belief that the saving work of Jesus Christ is a key not only to understanding Orthodox Christianity, but also to fulfilling the purpose of our human life.

I urge the reader to sit at the feet of this spiritual man and listen to the way he presents the faith of the New Testament in the context of our Christian life in the Church and how he evaluates the secular milieu in which we live. Attend to the sensitive, gentle, and concerned way in which he guides us to understanding.

Reading this book is a spiritual experience which conveys a quiet spiritual assurance. It reflects the man, whose presence, even when unaccompanied by words, does the same thing. I believe that I express the feelings of all who know Bishop Gerasimos and who read this book when I offer thanks to God for the gift He has given to us in Bishop Gerasimos and his writings.

Fr. Stanley S. Harakas

PROLOGUE

"Know the truth, and the truth will make you free..." (Jn. 8:32)

    Every person, especially a Christian, needs to know the truth as much as one possibly can. And every laborer of the Gospel will always feel the need to offer something for the truth of Christ. The Lord said: "Go therefore and make disciples of all nations" (Mt. 28:19). St. Paul, who was privileged to see the risen Lord personally, considered himself obliged to preach the Gospel of Christ to the Jews and to the Greeks, to the wise, and to the barbarians as well. "Woe to me if I do not preach the gospel!" (1 Cor. 9:16 f; cf. Rom. 1:14-17).

    So many books and films today obscure and distort the truth about God and man. And a good religious book will always be needed to shed some light like a small candle in the darkness of life. So much is written today by so many men of inspiration, and yet the Gospel of the Incarnate Christ will always be the only new thing in the world. And Christ will remain the light that illumines every person who desires to know the truth, for indeed He is "the light, the truth and the life" (Jn. 8:12; 14:6).

The new element in every contribution to the truth is how one approaches the manifold truth of faith in Christ. For whom does one write and how does one communicate to others that which he himself has understood in his mind and felt in his heart (1 Jn. 1:4). In my previous book, Orthodoxy Faith & Life, I expressed a general view of our faith as we live it in Sacred Scripture and in the life of the Church. In this book, I have developed certain reflections on the mystery of our Lord Jesus Christ: simple thoughts without scholarly observations, which do not, after all, provide much help in our personal life of faith. Sacred Scripture itself presents the truth simply, without too many questions and unnecessary explanations. When you take a passage of Scripture, read it carefully and meditate upon it. This will nourish and enlighten you spiritually. The study of Sacred Scripture of course presupposes the faith of the reader, and this faith is in turn enriched by such study.

The reflections contained in this book are an outpouring of my heart after many years of study, prayer, and meditation. They are an offering of love for all those who are seeking to grow in the image and likeness of our Lord and Savior Jesus Christ.

I wish to take this opportunity to thank those who have helped me prepare this book for publication: His Excellency Metropolitan Demetrios Trakatellis of Vresthena for reading the manuscript and making valuable suggestions; the Rev. Dr. Stanley S. Harakas for his contribution of the Preface; and the Rev. Deacon Constantine Newman for reading some sections of the manuscript. Also, I wish to thank Fr. Peter A. Chamberas for his tireless efforts to translate the Greek manuscript, prepare several revisions, and typeset the final edition for publication.

GERASIMOS

BISHOP OF ABYDOS

1910-1995

"ΈΜΟΙ ΓΑΡ ΤΟ ΖΗΝ

ΧΡΙΣΤΟΣ ΚΑΙ ΤΟ ΑΠΟΞ ΑΝΙΝ ΚΕΡΔΟΣ"

"FOR ME TO LIVE IS CHRIST AND TO DIE IS GAIN"

(PHIL 1:21)

A. INTRODUCTORY REFLECTIONS

1. *The Spirituality of Man*

Man is a unique being in the created world. He is created to be rational, free, and independent. Faith says that man is created in the image and likeness of God. It is in man that we can see the image of God. We have seen the real image of God in the Person of the God-Man Christ. It is the goal of man to be conformed to the image of Christ (Rom. 8:29; cf. Heb. 2:6-8). Man stands at the borderline of the uncreated, the invisible, and the divine, although he is created, visible, and human. Man has in his being the breath of God, the supernatural, and is always seeking something that is higher, that is better and perfect. While living in the world, man has his orientation toward God who is his archetype and his source of life. In fact, man lives and has his true being as long as he is oriented toward God (Acts 17:22-28). And his ultimate purpose is to meet God, to be united with Him, to achieve the likeness of God, "to acquire the Holy Spirit" of God.

The Greek philosophers saw man in this manner also, as desiring and seeking God, the highest good, the first cause, and as attempting to become similar to God to the extent possible for man. Without God as his Father, no matter what great things one achieves, man will always remain sadly an orphan and a stranger, lost in this vast, temporal and strange world. For man to truly live he needs something sublime, something steadfast and eternal. He wants the "ὄντως ὄν" (ontos on), as Plato would say, that which is by nature and essence true and beautiful in itself. And this is found only in God and in the godly life of man.

Even those who do not want a personal God, a creator, usually fashion some idol-god, reflecting their own weaknesses, to explain the mystery that is hidden in the world and in the heart of man. They worship themselves as god, despite humanity being too small and insignificant to be a god. This is by no means something new. From the beginning of creation, man has had the tendency to make himself god (Gen. 3:4-7). Others again deny God because they lose themselves in the theory of evolution. They seek to find the laws of evolution and forget that the laws themselves presuppose a mind that determines these laws.

A. INTRODUCTORY REFLECTIONS

Correct religion and correct science never come into conflict. The subject of science is different from the subject of faith. Science, moved by the power and the beauty of nature, seeks to discover the laws that are at work to create that beauty. Faith, on the other hand, takes the world for granted, but it too marvels at the beauty and power of the world. Moreover, faith sees behind this beauty the God who created the world, and proceeds to examine the relationship that exists between God the creator and the world, and particularly the relationship between God and man, "created in the image and likeness of God." Science cannot enter this subject of the spiritual relationship of man to God. The subject itself does not belong to its field of research. True faith itself cannot interfere in the subjects of science which have been clearly confirmed. Religion and science can enlighten each other without each entering into one another's Realms.

Science will always be searching, while faith that knows the truth by revelation will declare: "In the beginning was the Word ... and all things were made through him..."(Jn. 1:1-3). "In the beginning, God created the heavens and the earth..." and man was created in the image and likeness of God (Gen. 1:1 f, 1:27; Rom. 11:33-36; 1 Cor. 8:6). The scientist says, "I believe this or that." The person of faith says, "I believe in God." This latter statement implies involvement; it means establishing a relationship with God. A scientific man is not a complete person, without the mystery of faith in God, without a relationship with God in his or her life.

Behind the infinite world of law and order, faith sees God as the creator and governor of the world. He is a personal God with a mind, in the image of man we could say, since God created man to be a person in the image and likeness of God. Man wants God to be personal, to come into communion with him, to be concerned with his problems, and not to be some absolute and unknown being or power. This is what man seeks, and the Christian faith has given us these things in such a way that they can satisfy every soul that thirsts for light and truth. This is why Christ can say: "I am the way, and the truth, and the life" and "You will know the truth, and the truth will make you free" (Jn. 14:6; 8:32). For indeed the Truth is a Person; the Incarnate Son of God and our Lord and Savior Jesus Christ is the Truth.

2. *The Revelation of God*

We know God only by revelation. God is infinite, immaterial, and uncreated, and the created mind of man cannot comprehend Him. Only faith knows God, and only to the extent that He is revealed to us; to the extent that He comes to us in His energies, as the Church expresses it. God is a living personal being, acting, caring, moving within Himself, but also beyond Himself (ad extra.). In His love, God comes out of His self-sufficiency and blessedness and acts for the creation and salvation of the world. While God is invisible and cannot be known rationally, He is not

A. INTRODUCTORY REFLECTIONS

a stranger to the world, or "in him, we live and move and have our being"(Acts 17:28). God comes to us and speaks to us about Himself through His energies and actions. He speaks to us in many different ways and is revealed to us in different degrees. And first of all, God speaks to us in the beauty and harmony of His creation. "The heavens declare the glory of God" (Ps. 19:1) and all of the infinite world is a book of God that speaks to us about "his eternal power and deity" (Rom. 1:20; Acts 14:17). Ancient people worshiped the sun, the beautiful trees, or the powerful waterfalls because behind their beauty they could discern the presence of the power, the beauty, and the wisdom of the unknown God.

God, however, speaks much more to the heart of man. There in the heart of man, the meeting and the personal communication between man and God takes place. But for someone to hear the voice of God behind the infinite world of law and order and in our heart, there is need for an open heart, strong faith, and spiritual life, prayer, and worship. "The pure in heart shall see God" (Mt. 5:8). When our heart is pure, then we can see the image of God in us and can begin a dialogue with Him. In the Old Testament, we have many theophanies and conversations of man with God (cf. Gen. 18; Is. 6). Most especially however God spoke to us in Christ. Only Christ, the only begotten Son, and Logos of God knows the Father. "No one has ever seen God; the only begotten Son, who is in the bosom of the Father, he has made him known" (Jn. 1:18; Mt. 11:27).

Man is a communal being who needs communion and dialogue with his fellow human beings and even more so with God. Sacred Scripture and the Church describe the life of faith as a love relationship between man and God. The Church is presented as the bride of God or of Christ. And every soul is considered to be a bride to Christ (Mt. 22:37; cf. S. of S; Rev. 11,9-10). With fervent faith and love the great men of faith were able to come closer to God; they were privileged to see the glory of God, the divine light, in a perceptible manner (Mt. 17:1-8; Is. 6:1 f; Ezek. 33:18 f; 2 Cor. 12:1-4). These men first of all came to know God directly and personally, and then they were also able to speak to us about God and Christ in order for us also to believe and to have eternal life (Jn. 20:31; 1 Jn. 1:1-4; 5:12).

3. Faith and Knowledge

For someone to have faith and to live by that faith one must know what he believes. Faith and knowledge go together. The question, "Do you understand what you are reading?" is addressed to us as well by Philip (Acts 8:30). In essence, faith is life, communion with the God one believes in. Do we know well the content of our faith? Our problem today is that for so many people faith is considered as something secondary and irrelevant to life's daily needs. Consequently, we make little effort to learn more of the truth and thus do not experience the

A. INTRODUCTORY REFLECTIONS

full power and beauty that faith provides for our daily life. We do not keep "the first love" of faith. Faith does not cause "our hearts to burn within us", and it is not expressed in a living manner in our daily life (Rev. 2:4; Lk. 24,32). Many times our faith is choked by the thorns of daily life and does not bear "much fruit" (Mt. 13:22-23; Gal. 5:22-23). It is, therefore, necessary not only to learn about our faith, but also to live by our faith and our communion with God so that we may experience its power and its beauty.

4. Faith and the Church

Faith is life, the life of the Church. Both religion and theology are a product of the Church, of the people of God, and not of a group nor of individuals. Faith is the life of the people. And in our case, it is the life experience of our salvation in the Person of Christ. The Apostles, as individuals, expressed their own ideas on our faith, but the faith in Christ was already lived from the very beginning by the whole Church community. The Apostles spoke on behalf of the whole community.

The theologian today is called to build on this foundation of faith. One must penetrate deeply into the given faith, live the deeper meaning of the words of Scripture, and project that meaning for the building up of the community of faith. The theologian must build upon the delivered faith, and never create a new faith according to his own convictions. We are called to theologize upon the given revelation and not to philosophize according to our own understandings; nor should we ever seek to impose such understandings upon the life of the Church.

The foundation in the life of the Church is the experience of our salvation in Jesus Christ, and not the temporary philosophical or cultural ideas of individuals. Faith is not against human life, but it is there to illumine the life of the centuries and not to be interpreted by worldly theories. The Church, above all, speaks about redemption and the kingdom of God. This idea of the kingdom of God can illumine and direct the many other problems and issues of life. The final goal of our world is to become a kingdom of God, a kingdom of faith and love within the great and infinite love of God.

B. THE MYSTERY OF THE DIVINE PLAN

OF SALVATION IN CHRIST

The difficult aspect of Christian faith is the mystery of salvation in Christ. Everyone can believe, more or less, in an indefinite and generalized idea about God (Rom. 1:20). The indefinite does not restrict us in our thoughts and deeds. But this is not the case with the Christian faith, which is based on the mystery of the Person of Christ. Faith here is concrete; it depends upon what Christ revealed to us about God. Faith in God depends on our faith in the Person and the work of Christ. And the work of Christ again depends upon what we believe about God. God and Christ are known mutually. If one does not believe in God he does not believe in Christ either. And if one does not believe in Christ he does not believe in the true God either (Mt. 11:27; Lk. 10:22; Jn. 1:18; 10:15). The God we believe in is "the God and Father of our Lord Jesus Christ" (Rom. 15:6; 2 Cor. 1:3). In the first article of the Creed, we confess: "I believe in one God, the Father, the Almighty, creator of heaven and earth..." Once we truly believe in God as creator and Father, all the other doctrines of the faith are easy. Everything in our faith is an "interpretation" of the first article of the creed. If you believe and understand in your heart that God is Father, that He loves the world He created, and that He speaks to and guides His children through His prophets, then it is easy to believe that God can also find a way to condescend and, if necessary, become man to save His children who are in danger of being lost. And all of this faith St. John was able to capture in one single verse: "For God so loved the world that he gave his only Son, that whoever believes in him should not perish but have eternal life" (Jn. 3:16).

This is primarily what Christ brought to us: that God is truly Father, and as Father, He loves and cares for His children. Christ came as the love of God, to seek and to save the lost, to call us all back to the love of God, to the kingdom of God for which we were created in the first place (Mt. 25:34). This the Church has called "the mystery of the economy (the plan) of God in Christ." And this is the heart of our faith.

1. A Hidden Mystery

The Gospel presents to us salvation in Christ as a mystery hidden in the eternal will of God. In a sense, all things in life

B. THE MYSTERY OF THE DIVINE PLAN OF SALVATION IN CHRIST

are a mystery, the flowers, the birds, the stars, life itself, history, regardless of how simple and readily comprehensible they may seem at first sight. The subject of faith, however, is much more difficult and more mysterious, for it involves God and His work, as well as man, who believes in God. Our Lord Jesus Christ is especially a mystery that transcends the mind of man. We come to know Christ only by revelation, as much as God reveals Him to us, and as much as man accepts Him in faith and with a believing heart. And even then Christ remains a mystery, far above any intellectual knowledge and understanding.

In Christ we have the revelation of God par excellence only at the Parousia, that is, the Second Coming of Christ, with the perfection of all things, will we have another revelation. In the Old Testament, we see God providing for His people with love. In Christ, we see God as eternal love who cares, and who, as a concerned Father, condescends to the suffering of man. He becomes man to help man ascend to God so that man might again become a son of God, as he was created and destined to be. This is how the Church understood the mystery of Christ, particularly St. John and St. Paul (Jn. 3:16; 1 Jn. 4:7-12; Rom. 8:35-39). If we do not see God as love condescending to His creatures, we are not yet Christians, we do not yet believe in the true God-Father. This mystery of Christ had remained hidden and silent in the eternal will of God, unknown even to the angels. Everything that pertains to God, thoughts, and actions, is to be understood as being eternal, outside of the limitations of time and space. They all exist in an eternal present as far as God is concerned. But we come to see them and understand them when they are realized in history. The Apostles and the Fathers see Christ as the eternal Word of God "through whom all things were made." He was even present in the deceit and actively brought about the marvelous events in the history of Israel (Jn. 1:1-3; 1 Cor. 10:4,11).

In the Old Testament, we had only certain signs, types, and symbols of what was to be in the future (Heb. 7:18-19; 10:1). All of these were preparing the world to accept the Messiah-Savior. And all the religions and the philosophies of that time were expecting a Messiah-Savior. The Patriarchs and the Prophets of the Old Testament lived with the hope of the coming of the Messiah. They sought to learn at what time the suffering and the glory of the Messiah would take place (1 Pet. 1:10-11). Everything regarding Christ takes place "according to the Scriptures," "that Scripture may be fulfilled" (Mt. 1:22; 4:14; Lk. 24:26-44; 1 Pet. 1:10-12). This is the new thing in the Gospel of Christ. In the Person of Christ and in the founding of the Church, the hopes and expectations of Israel were fulfilled. The eternal plan of God for the salvation of the world in Christ was realized. "For Christ is the end of the law unto righteousness for everyone who believes" (Rom. 10:4). The main purpose of Israel was to prepare the world to believe in Christ and to be saved. And indeed Israel prepared the world for the reception of Christ. The Church now considers itself to be the New Israel of God (Gal. 6:16).

B. THE MYSTERY OF THE DIVINE PLAN OF SALVATION IN CHRIST

2. *The Person and the Work of Christ*

The Person of Christ is the foundation and heart of the Christian faith. Christology is also soteriology, that is, the doctrine of the Person of Christ is also the doctrine of our salvation. A Christian is one who believes in Christ as Savior, as Lord and God one who believes and feels that he belongs to Christ and is saved by Him. It is therefore very important and certainly worthwhile to think about and to approach the mystery of Christ with our mind too, as far as it is possible for man. First of all, we must keep in mind that the Person of Christ in our faith is a great mystery connected to the mystery of God, of man, and the world. The mystery of Christ illumines the many obscure points of life and of the history of the world. Christ is a mystery that is to be understood in another mystery, that of the Church, which again is the mystery of our salvation in Christ. The Apostles and the Church generally understood Christ in terms of the salvation of the world. And this salvation was understood as a work of the love of God for us, as it is clearly expressed in Jn. 3:16, but also as a response of our own love for God and Christ (Jn. 14:15-26; 17:17-23; Mk. 10:48; Rom. 5:8; 8:31-39). This is the real message of the New Testament Church. Christ can be understood only in the context of the experience of the redeemed Church. And as St. Paul says, in order to understand the mystery, we must believe; we must have a heart rooted deeply in faith and in the love of Christ; we must believe and live Christ within the life of the redeemed Church, "together with all of the saints" (Eph. 3:14-19). Apart from the Church, as individuals and with rational thought alone, we cannot approach this mystery of Christ; it transcends our finite mind. Only the redeemed Church can approach the mystery; and this only as an experience of salvation. Only when we experience the forgiving divine love, when we find ourselves in the realm of divine grace, can we understand and experience how God knows us and recognizes us as His children, and how He works and becomes man to save us. The more we accept the love of God and the more we purify our heart, the more we understand the mystery of divine love. When one feels and believes that God loves the world and is concerned for man, then one can easily understand and believe also the mystery of Christ, even if this is accomplished, as the Fathers have noted, as a mystery beyond knowledge. "I believe in order to understand, and not, I understand in order to believe"(-Jn. 6:69; Augustine).

3. "Who Do Men Say That I Am?" (Mk. 8:27).

This question was posed by Christ to His disciples shortly before His Crucifixion. Through His disciples, the question is posed to all of us: "Who do you say that I am?" (Mt. 16:15; Mk. 8:29; Lk. 9:20). Our faith in and response to Christ is a personal matter that requires a personal answer that is both responsible and sincere. You, a rational being created in the image of God, can declare who Christ is, who God is, who man is. You can and must confess responsibly from your heart, what

B. THE MYSTERY OF THE DIVINE PLAN OF SALVATION IN CHRIST

exactly you believe about the Person of Christ. Each person must approach Christ personally; one must touch Him, know Him, and make a responsible decision about Him. Any attempt to avoid an answer to this question betrays indifference and unbelief (cf. Jn. 20:31; Rom. 10:8-18).

Jesus, Christ, Son of God, Son of Man, Word-Logos

The Apostles and the people recognized Jesus, on the basis of His teaching and His works, as the expected Messiah-Savior, as the Son of God (cf. Lk. 1:35; Mt. 3:17; 17:5). But Christ was not simply a descendant of David. He was a divine Person, the Lord of David. He was the Son of Man that Daniel had a vision of as the Savior of the world (Dan. 7, 13-14; Mk. 12:35-37). This is what Jesus Himself emphasized when He spoke about Himself as the judge and the savior. He had authority to forgive sins and to give life (Mt. 9:3; Jn. 5:26-27).

In the Person of Jesus Christ, St. John sees the eternal Logos of God and God "through whom all things were made." "And the Logos became flesh." Now the Incarnate Logos-God is the eternal Son of God, full of grace and truth (Jn. 1:1, 14-18). According to the Fathers, St. John called the Son Logos in order to show that the generation of the Son is not passive, as is that of men. He also wanted to show the close relationship of the Son with the Father. The Father and the Son are united into one, as the mind and the word are one. Moreover, the Son is the Logos, the Word because He proclaims to the people the good news; He reveals God to mankind. Everyone who knows and understands the Son also understands the Father who has begotten Him (Jn. 14:6-11; Irenaeus, IV,6,6).

With the expression, "in the beginning he was", St. John denotes the eternity of the Son. All creation has its beginning. The Son was in the beginning with the Father, eternal and co-equal to the Father. And "everything was made through him." And it is through Him also that we receive our salvation.

And in time the Word became flesh and we beheld His glory, which is a glory that only the only begotten Son of God can have, "full of grace and truth."

Thus the Jesus of Nazareth, the Jesus of the Church is the Christ, the Son of God and the Son of Man, the Son of God par excellence and the Savior of the world. It is about this Christ that the Apostles write of, expressing themselves freely, and it is this Christ that the believing Church knows.

Peter first confessed on behalf of the Apostles that Jesus of Nazareth is the Christ, the expected Messiah, and Savior. After the Resurrection and Pentecost, with the illumination of the Holy Spirit, the Apostles taught us the truth about the Person of Christ as Savior, Lord, and God. In just a few but powerful lines, they describe for us how they lived Christ during

B. THE MYSTERY OF THE DIVINE PLAN OF SALVATION IN CHRIST

His earthly presence, and how the Church experienced Him after the Resurrection in its preaching and worship, in Baptism, and in the holy Eucharist.

Christ is the Son of the living God. As God, Christ exists eternally "in the form of God," but in time became man for us, taking "the form of a servant". "In Him dwells the whole fullness of the deity." He is the eternal Logos of God and God "through whom all things were made." In time He became man and walked among us. "We have beheld his glory, glory as of the only Son from the Father, full of grace and truth" (Phil. 2:6-11; Col. 2:9; Jn. 1:1-18; Acts 9:1-9; 26:13).

As God Incarnate Christ lived, taught, healed, raised the dead, and completed His work upon the Cross. It was there on the Cross that He uttered the final word: "It is finished," τετέλεσται (tetelestai) that is to say, "the work given to me is accomplished." With love and obedience unto death to the will of God, Christ conquered sin and death. As victor, He rose, ascended, sat at the right hand of God the Father, and in the Holy Spirit governs the Church until the end of the world. Another clearer confession of faith is that of Thomas: "My Lord and my God!" (Jn. 1:1.14; 20:28; Phil. 2:6-11; Mt. 28:18-20). Thomas made faith in Christ complete.

This particular faith of the Apostles was saved and transmitted to us as historical events, as religious experience of the Church lived in its preaching and worship of the Incarnate Christ, without any rational explanation of the mystery.

Later when some people attempted to understand the mystery with human logic, with their own presuppositions, and outside the realm of the Church's faith, then the Fathers of the Church undertook the struggle to define the right and correct faith of the Church, and thus to protect it from the danger of deviations and heresies. Based on revelation, the early tradition of the Apostles, and the ongoing practice of the Church, they defined and established the faith of the Church in the Person of Christ as Theanthropos (God-Man), Lord, God, and Savior of the world. And this they defined as a revealed mystery and never as human knowledge. They sought to show that the mystery is neither rational nor irrational, but rather supernatural. One marvels even today at how much attention the Apostles and the Fathers emphasized the reality of both the divinity and the humanity of the Incarnate Christ: Son of God and Son of David in the flesh; Jesus the man and Jesus the Lord. The climax of this definition of the faith in Christ is in the doctrinal formulation of the Fourth Ecumenical Council at Chalcedon (451 A.D.).

The eternal Logos became man in time and came to be with us. He became man in order to raise man up to God. He is not from among us; He came from God the Father. Christ came and completed the work which the Father had given Him, and again He returned to the Father.

The how of the Incarnation belongs to the profound mystery of the Holy Trinity. Therefore, we need to express a few thoughts and reflections on the Holy Trinity.

B. THE MYSTERY OF THE DIVINE PLAN OF SALVATION IN CHRIST

4. The Mystery of the Holy Trinity

Man, as the image of God, seeks by nature to know God and to speak to Him personally as a son to a father. There in communion with God man finds the perfection his soul yearns; he finds the holy and his true being. This searching distinguishes man from all the other creatures (Mt. 4:4; Acts 17:27-28). The soul of man is created for God and it cannot rest until man finds himself in God. God, however, is the Holy One, the totally Other, and man has never been able to see God "face to face" and to know what God is (Ex. 33:11-23).

In the New Testament, God is one, with one will and energy. But He exists and reveals Himself in three divine Persons who bring about the salvation of the world. And the Church believes that while God is one in essence, He is revealed in three Hypostases or Persons. How the immaterial and invisible God exists in three Persons, what is the relationship of the three Persons in the inner life of God, and how the eternal Triune God acts outside of Himself in time (ad extra) to create and to recreate the world: these are questions that will remain an untouchable mystery for finite man. The Church says simply this: "God is infinite and incomprehensible, and only this can be known about Him, namely, His infinity and incomprehensibility" (St. Gregory the Theologian, P.G. 36,628A). God is infinite, and the finite mind of man cannot contain Him. This is the appropriate self-awareness of rational man, that he is a limited creature and not God, unable to enter the mystery of the inner life of God and to know the interrelationship of the three Persons and the way God is working ad extra for His world. We know that God is and what He does for the world, but not what He is in essence. A God fully-known and understood by man is no longer God. He becomes an object, an "it", to be studied and handled by man. God is Spirit, beyond being, and the source of every being in the world. He is in all and contains all things, but He is not contained by anything. Whatever one says about God is merely an attempt to approach a mystery. Man is overwhelmed and loses his mind if he should dare alone to understand God. God is the Transcendent One, the totally Other, inapproachable to the created mind. We know God only to the extent that we seek Him with awe and love. This seeking within us is a sort of proof of His existence and His presence within us. We know God as He is revealed in the majesty of nature and in our open heart. Our faith is our personal response to His whispering in our heart through the beauty of the world. God is a living and acting Person. He lives in Himself in an eternal love relationship as Father, Son, and Holy Spirit, and He reveals Himself as He comes to us in His actions for the creation and salvation of the world.

God reveals Himself to spiritual, pious, and virtuous people, persons with open hearts and minds. There is a person-to-person communion in which God reveals to His friends His existence and His holy will for the world. There in the presence of God, embraced by the majesty, glory, and holiness of God, man ceases to

B. THE MYSTERY OF THE DIVINE PLAN OF SALVATION IN CHRIST

speak and to ask questions about what and how. He only listens to the voice of God, and with fear, faith, and love says: "Speak (Lord) for thy servant is listening" (Gen. 3:1; 1 Sam. 3:10; Is. 6:8; Acts 9). Then and only then a man can speak about God as Samuel, Abraham, Moses, Peter, Paul, and others have spoken. God used to speak to Moses face to face, as man speaks to his friend (Gen. 18:22-33. Ex. 33:11).

In the divine economy in Christ, however, God has revealed Himself fully. God has addressed us in His Logos, in the Person of His Son, Jesus Christ (Heb. 1:3; Jn. 1:18). We have really seen and heard God speaking to us in person (Jn. 14:6-11). As St. Irenaeus says: "The Father is the invisible (part) of the Son, but the Son is the visible of the Father..." (Adv. haer. IV 6,6). Christ is the exact or physical image of God and we become images of Christ (Col. 1:15; 1 Cor. 15:49; Rm. 8:29). In the Incarnate Son, we have seen that God is Trinity, that God the Father creates and saves everything in the world through the Son, and the Holy Spirit completes the work. Out of love the Son and Logos of God condescends and becomes man in Christ to help man become a child of God, god by grace. And the Holy Spirit fulfills the task of salvation in the Church. The Church from the very beginning has believed and confessed that God in essence is one, but in three hypostases or Persons, Father, Son, and Holy Spirit, as revealed in the commandment of the risen Christ (Mt. 28:19). This is how we see God in His working ad extra for the creation and salvation of the world, but never in His essence and inner being, living in His unfathomable eternity (Jn. 14:9-10, 16-17; 1 Jn. 4:2).

The names Father, Son, and Holy Spirit must not be understood in a human way. Rather, they present the way of the existence of the One God in a relationship of three Persons in the one Divinity. The three are the one God. They are spirit and as spirit, they indwell each other.

Each of the three Persons possesses complete divinity, for divinity is unique and undivided. Three perfections are united in one God: three in one and one in three, in a perfect union of love. "No sooner do I conceive of the One that I am illumined by the splendor of the Three. No sooner do I distinguish them that I am carried back to the One. When I think of any one of the Three I think of Him as a whole" (St. Gregory the Theologian, P.G. 36,417B). One has to surpass the human way of thinking to reach the contemplation of a reality beyond human intelligence to see the One in the Three and the Three in the One (Greg. Theol. P.G. 35,1160C-1161C). Essence and hypostases are not a division, but rather a reflection of the mysterious life of the one God. We are not speaking in a human way about a first, second, or third God. We adore God as God, confessing the individuality of the hypostases (St. Basil, P.G. 32,149B, cf. V. Lossky, The Vision of God, p. 46-48). The Father receives a greater emphasis because He is the original source and cause of divinity. It is in the Father that we see the oneness of the Holy

B. THE MYSTERY OF THE DIVINE PLAN OF SALVATION IN CHRIST

Trinity. But the Three Persons are co-eternal and co-equal; one God, one essence and nature; one will and energy; one work ad extra, for the creation and salvation of the world.

St. Gregory the Theologian sees the revelation of the Triune God in three stages: First, from the Mosaic Law, we learned about the one God, the Father, but only faintly about the Son. Second, the New Testament manifested the Son and intimated the divinity of the Holy Spirit. Third, in the period of the Holy Spirit, we receive the good news of our transference from here to eternity (P.G. 36,164C). The Church says: The Father, through the Son, in the Holy Spirit creates everything. More liberally, the Church Fathers may say: God the Father with His Two Hands (the Son and the Holy Spirit) creates everything. Or to put it still another way: God the Father as Mind, through the Word, in the Holy Spirit creates and saves the world (Irenaeus, IV,4,20; Athanasios, P.G. 26,212C).

While the Church Fathers dare to express themselves in this manner for the work of God ad extra, as we have seen God working our salvation in Christ, no one dared to enter the unfathomable mystery of the essence of God and the movements in the inner life of the Holy Trinity. The mystery of The Holy Trinity has been revealed only in the divine plan and action of salvation, and only as a revelation in mystery and never as human understanding.

Why Three Persons?

Just because we have seen God working our salvation in this way. God the Father has the will to save the world; the Son puts the will of the Father into action. The Son became man to realize the will of the Father, to save the world by His Cross and Resurrection (Mt. 3:17; Jn. 4:34; Heb. 10:7). The Holy Spirit completes the work of salvation throughout history in the Church. One more thing that we could say is that God is a Person and a person only exists in communion with other persons. The communion of three -- I-thou-he -- is the perfect communion. This is the mode or the way of existence of the one God, Holy Trinity.

The Three Persons in the Holy Trinity

The Father

When we say simply "God" our mind goes to God the Father of the first article of our faith. Once we believe in God as Father, creator, and almighty, then all the themes of faith become easier to understand. In the Person of the Father, we have the Oneness and the Trinity of God. God the Father eternally begets the Son and causes the Holy Spirit to proceed eternally.

The Son of God

"And I believe in one Lord, Jesus Christ, the only begotten Son of God..." The goal of the world is its salvation, and the salvation of the world is to become the kingdom of

B. THE MYSTERY OF THE DIVINE PLAN OF SALVATION IN CHRIST

God. The center of our salvation is the Person of Christ. In the Person of Christ, we have seen and known the Father, and have reached our salvation. Christ, therefore, has a central place in our faith.

In the Old Testament we have no clear reference to the Son of God, but only types and symbols of the beloved Servant of God. Son of God is a name used for Israel as the beloved people of God (Ex. 4:22. Hos. 11:1). Son of God is also a title of the king, and especially of the expected Messiah-King (Gen. 18:18; 22:18; Is. 9:6; Ps. 2:7). The angel announced Jesus as the expected Messiah-Savior (Lk. 1:32, 54-55; Mt. 3:11, 11:3; Jn. 11:27). The Evangelists try to prove that Jesus the Messiah had to be glorified through His Passion (Lk. 24:26. Acts 17:3, 26:23).

The Son of Man

Speaking of Himself, Christ often used the term Son of Man, as someone coming in the clouds, thus indicating He is from above and has royal authority and judgment over the whole world (Mt. 19:27, 25:31; Mk. 14:61-62; Jn. 5:21-27).

"Born of the Holy Spirit."

Christ is the expected Messiah King, but He is different from king David and from any king. He is unique. His conception is divine. "The Holy Spirit will come upon you, and the power of the Most High will overshadow you; therefore the child to be born will be called holy, the son of God" (Lk. 1:35; cf. 3:33-38). This is the first testimony that Christ is indeed the Son of God (cf. Mt. 3:17, 16:16, 17:5; Jn. 5:18, 19:7).

The Son and Logos of God

The faith of the Church has been established and the believers live their faith in Christ in the liturgical and doxological life of prayer and praise (Jn. 3:5, 6:51-57; 2 Cor. 10:16-17. 11, 23-26). St. John, inspired by the Holy Spirit, the Spirit of truth (Jn. 15:26, 16:13) writes the famous Prologue of his Gospel where he expresses the faith of the Church in the Person of Jesus Christ. "In the beginning was the Word and the Word was with God, and the Word was God... all things were made through Him... In him was life and the life was the light of men" (Jn. 1:1-4). The Word is God (not just divine), and He is always with God. Everything in the world comes into being by the Word of God and all have their life and light in Him. The life of men takes its meaning in Him and without Him, everything lies in darkness and is darkness (Jn. 1:5-9).

"And the Word Became Flesh" (Jn. 1:14)

The eternal Word, at a certain time in history, took flesh (humanity from the Virgin Mary) and became fully and truly man, and was not simply an inspiration to Jesus Christ. As true and whole man, He has walked and dwelt among us, and "we have beheld his glory, glory as of the only Son from the Father, full of grace and truth" (Jn. 1:14).

B. THE MYSTERY OF THE DIVINE PLAN OF SALVATION IN CHRIST

The Word-Logos-Son of God

What is the Word Logos of God? So many things have been said about the Logos in the Greek world, as the mind of God or even as God governing the world.

St. John knew the Word of God in the creation of the world. "God said let there be light, and there was light" (Gen. 1:3, 1 Cor. 4:4-6). Another word is the Word of God given to the prophets to instruct and guide the people. The Word of Jesus Christ Himself is the Word of God that can give life or can judge the world (Jn. 5:24-30). In Christ God has spoken to us in person, in His Logos-Son.

The Eternal Son of God

In speaking about the Logos, St. John does not speak about a philosophical Logos; He speaks of the Person of Jesus Christ, whose glory he has beheld as the glory of the only Son of God. John the Baptist also came to witness for Jesus Christ and declared "that this is the Son of God" (Jn. 1:7-15, 34; 3:36; 20:31). John knew that Jesus Christ existed with the Father before Abraham and before the creation of the world (Jn. 8:58; 17:5-24), but now he sees Jesus Christ related to the eternal Logos of God. The Logos, the personal wisdom and creative power through whom God thinks and creates the world, became man in Jesus Christ. He who once created the world now became the saving power and wisdom of God (1 Cor. 1:25-30). Christ is the Incarnate Logos of God (Jn. 1-14). Once Christ is identified with the eternal Logos of God, He becomes the eternal Son of God. Faith sees everything in the eternal will, plan, and action of God (Jn. 3:21-25. Eph. 3:3-12). In the heart of John and of the Church the Jesus Christ of history, the Logos Incarnate, the Christ in the life of the Church now, the Christ of eternity in the hereafter, and the Logos before the Incarnation are seen as one Person within the eternity of God. In this eternal Logos-Christ, God is working for the salvation of the world, leading humanity to its final goal, to its sanctification and union with God in the perfected kingdom of God. Thus Jesus Christ, as the eternal Logos Incarnate, is the unique Son of God, the personal wisdom, mind, and power through whom God the Father creates and saves the world. He was and is always with God, "in the bosom of God." And in time He became man for the salvation of the world (Jn. 1:14-18).

"All things were made through him, and without him was not anything made that was made. In him was life, and the life was the light of men" (Jn. 1:3-4). Christ, as the Logos and Son of God has created everything. He is the source of life for every living creature in the world. The life He gives us is the light of man. Man is different from any other living creature in the world. He is created in the image of God. His purpose is to reach the likeness of God, to live eternally in communion with the eternal God. To reach this goal man needs a light to enlighten him and to guide him to live and to enjoy his life here on earth properly. And Christ, with his life and teaching, is the

B. THE MYSTERY OF THE DIVINE PLAN OF SALVATION IN CHRIST

true, the real light, which can give us a true, a real life, worthy of human beings, a life that leads man to reach the purpose for which he is created, to reach the likeness of God and life eternal (Jn. 17:3).

Christ, the eternal Son and Logos of God, is indeed the true light of the world (Jn. 1:9). He enlightened everyone before the Incarnation, during His life on earth, and through His Gospel, His light still "shines" in the darkness of the world (Jn. 1:5). Without Christ, our life does not reach its full meaning for the thinking man. We remain in darkness and are judged. Christ indeed came as life in the world. In the Person and teaching of Christ, human life reaches its perfection, its full meaning for the present time and for the future, with the hope of a closer communion with God in Jesus Christ (Jn. 1:4-5, 9; 8:12; 11:25-26; 12:35-46, 47; 14:6).

Christ gives light and life because He is the eternal Logos and Son of God, who is God (Jn. 1:1-20, 28-31). One needs faith and an open heart to meet Christ, to accept Him, to see His divine glory, and to be changed, becoming sons and daughters of light and children of God (Jn. 1:10-14; 12:36).

St. John used the term Logos-Word, as a familiar term known to many in his time, to lighten the eternal Father-Son relationship of Christ. From now on he speaks freely about Jesus Christ as the Son of God, as the absolute Son of God. The Gospel of John is the history of the Incarnate Logos-Son of God in the Person of Jesus Christ.

St. Paul sees the pre-existence of Christ in the same way as St. John. Christ was eternally "in the form of God... (in) equality with God" and in time became man. He took the "form of a servant" and died on the Cross for our salvation, and now is exalted and worshiped "in heaven, on earth, and under the earth," and every being confesses that Jesus Christ, the Theanthropos, is Lord of the universe, to the glory of God the Father (Phil. 2:6-11; Gal. 4:4-6; Col. 1:19; 2:9).

The Fathers can see Christ the Logos Incarnate as the archetype for the creation of man, and the final goal of man is to become Christ-like, to be conformed to the image of Christ (Rom. 8:29). This is the mystery of Christ, the Word-Logos of God, who became man to save mankind and the world. He is the Messiah-King, the Savior, the Son of God par excellence the second Person of the Holy Trinity. Jesus-Savior and Emmanuel-God is with us, is His name because He is the God-Man, King and Archpriest of mankind.

The Holy Spirit

The Holy Spirit is the third Person of the Holy Trinity, the "second hand" through whom the Father creates and saves the world. In Genesis 1:2 "the Holy Spirit was moving over the waters" (over the newly created world) as if He had hatched the "egg" (the formless and lifeless world) about to become alive (St. Basil).

B. THE MYSTERY OF THE DIVINE PLAN OF SALVATION IN CHRIST

The Holy Spirit is a Person. He spoke to the prophets, He inspires us, prays for us, distributes the gifts as He wills, and He grieves over our wrongdoings (Eph. 4:30; Acts 5:3-10). The Holy Spirit is worshiped and glorified together with the Father and the Son.

The Holy Spirit prepared the world through the prophets to receive the Savior; He prepared the Virgin to conceive the Savior and cooperated with Christ in His ministry. After the Resurrection Christ sent the Holy Spirit, or, we may say, the Father sent Him in the name of the Son. The Holy Spirit now abides in the Church and fulfills the work of salvation. He leads the people to Christ and thus realizes the kingdom of God on earth. In the Holy Spirit God is with us. The eternal kingdom of God will be the fullness of the presence of the Holy Spirit in us, the eternal glory of God among us.

5. *The Relationship of the Son and the Holy Spirit*

Some Fathers of the Church indicate that the Holy Spirit proceeds or is shown forth from the Father through the Son (through, and not from the Son, i.e. Filioque). The Scriptures speak about the Trinity from the point of view of the divine economy for our salvation, and not from their eternal interrelationship. Scripture presents both the Son and the Holy Spirit as divine Persons, eternal and homoousia, eternally being born or proceeding from God the Father for the salvation of the world.

In the divine plan enacted for our salvation, we could say that first the Son came and saved the world, and then the Holy Spirit came to us, manifested Himself to us. Our Lord presented this truth to His disciples the evening of the Mystical Supper. "I go to the Father... and I will pray the Father, and he will give you another Counselor to be with you forever, even the Spirit of truth... the Holy Spirit, whom the Father will send in my name; he will teach you all things, and bring to your remembrance all that I have said to you (Jn. 14:13-17, 26)... It is for your advantage that I go away, for if I do not go away, the Counselor will not come to you; but if I go, I will send him to you... He will glorify me, for he will take what is mine and declare it to you"(Jn. 16:5-7, 14). But we are not allowed to apply this interrelationship to the inner eternal life of God. No one can enter the abyss of the inner life of God. Therefore, the expression "through the Son" of some Fathers must have been influenced by the work of our salvation. For there, in the divine economy of salvation in Christ, we have seen and known the three Persons, Father, Son, and Holy Spirit.

The heart of the faith of the Church is that in the Person and work of Christ, the Incarnate divine Son and Logos was working, not just the man Jesus of Nazareth, even though the Logos of God became man. That is to say, "God was in

B. THE MYSTERY OF THE DIVINE PLAN OF SALVATION IN CHRIST

Christ reconciling the world to himself" (2 Cor. 5:19). And we see the Incarnate Son-Logos as the second Person of the Holy Trinity. When the salvation of the world, through the Passion and Resurrection of the Son of God, was completed once and for all time, then the Holy Spirit began His work of salvation. Therefore, avoiding the filioque controversy, we would say: In the divine plan of our salvation, the work of the Son was a necessary preparation for the Holy Spirit to start His work for the fulfillment of salvation.

The Holy Spirit, the Lord, and giver of life guides the faithful into "all the truth" about Christ and His work (Jn. 14:16-26; 15:26; 16:7-15). The Holy Spirit brings us to Christ; unites us with Christ and sanctifies us.

The Holy Spirit is the Spirit of God because He comes forth from the Father. He is also the Spirit of Christ since He is working on the work of salvation in Christ, which is the work of the Holy Trinity: "From the Father, through the Son, in the Holy Spirit."

This is the way the Church lives our salvation in Christ and our faith in the Holy Trinity. Do we understand all this with our mind? No! Only heretics and non-believers claim to know God with their mind. For the Church, all these are matters of faith, and matters of faith belong rather to the heart than to the mind. Man is both heart and mind. The radar of faith penetrates realms of reality where our mind can never enter. The pure heart can see God in the world, in itself, and in Christ. The mind cannot understand all the messages of the heart, but it cannot deny them either. The work of the mind is to accept the messages of the heart and to put them in some order so that we can receive their highest meaning for our life. These messages of the heart are always a matter of life and of a relationship of a higher level (1 Cor. 2:9-16; 2 Cor. 12:11-10).

All that is said and written in our Christian faith comes from the experience of our salvation in Christ and of the presence of the Holy Spirit who is working our salvation and sanctification in the Church. The Church lives the mystery of salvation in Christ as it received it from the Apostles in faith and worship, and not as a human knowledge or understanding. And everyone who has experienced his salvation in Christ and feels himself in the sphere of grace, can believe, understand, and live his salvation without questions about the how of the Holy Trinity, which will always remain a mystery to our mind. Faith is the life of the heart and communion with God, not knowledge of the mind.

If someone does not feel the need of salvation and does not feel the presence of divine love within and without himself, he is spiritually dead. He cannot believe and he cannot speak with certainty of God, nor of man, nor of anything else in the world, for everything exists in God (Jn. 14:6; Acts 17:28; Rom. 11:36).

B. THE MYSTERY OF THE DIVINE PLAN OF SALVATION IN CHRIST

6. The Incarnation

The heart of Christian faith is the mystery of the divine plan of salvation Christ. And the heart of the mystery of this divine plan is the Incarnation of the Son and Logos of God. This is the subject of the Gospel: God became man "for us and for our salvation" Jesus-Savior is his name, but also Emmanuel, which means (in Christ) God is with us. In Christ, we do not have so much a teaching about God, as we have the very presence of God Himself, a true theophany. In Christ God has spoken to us personally, in the Person of His Son (Mt. 1:20-25; Heb. 1:1-2; Jn. 1:18; 14:9; 2 Cor. 5:19-21). The Incarnation is a special event of God in history to help humanity find its way back to God.

With the Incarnation, we touch the mystery of God and how He is working outside Himself for the salvation of the world. The how of the Incarnation will remain a mystery. It is a matter of faith and, as we have said, faith is the life of the heart, not of the mind. The mind follows the experience of the heart and tries to get a glimpse of the mystery of God and man. To have an insight into the Incarnation we must have a better understanding of God and man, and the God-man relationship; what the life of God is, and what the life of man is, and how it can be united with God and be sanctified and deified. The only thing the Church could say concerning the mystery of the Incarnation is that man is not a stranger to God. He is created by God, in the image and likeness of God; man is a microcosm, and potentially a microtheos. Man is not far from God, "for in Him we live and move and are" (Acts 17:27-28). The basic difference between man and God is that man is a creature and God is the creator. God is the absolute Spirit-Person. He lives and acts and is in relationship with the world and especially with human beings. Man is a limited, created spiritual person who lives a creature-creator relationship with God. We live in God and share His love. Man is a unique creature, the only spiritual being in the world. He is created in the image of God, similar to God, and capable of knowing God and being known by God, and living in communion with God (Jn. 17:3-23; 1 Cor. 8:3). Only man can know God and only in the pure heart of man can one see the image of God, what God looks like. Man has received the breath of God, and we live as we share in the life of God.

The Logos is in essence outside of all, but in all according to His energies or activities; He penetrates and gives life to everything (Jn. 1:3). Out of love, the eternal God comes out of His eternal blessedness, and in His Son-Logos becomes man. The Logos, who in the beginning created man according to His image, could and did receive a human nature and became man, without separating Himself from His divine nature. Man himself, created in the image and likeness of God, can receive the divine Logos. Now, as God-Man, the Son can be everywhere: He can be "as Son to the Father and as Logos to the world giving life to everything" (St. Athanasios, P.G. 25,125). He can be in the

B. THE MYSTERY OF THE DIVINE PLAN OF SALVATION IN CHRIST

bosom of the Father and in the arms of the Mother; "on the throne in heaven, and on the cross for us." As God-Man He can sit at the right hand of God the Father, and be with us in Spirit "to the close of the age." Also, as we say in the Divine Liturgy: Christ is "sitting above with the Father and invisibly present here with us."

"When the Time Had Fully Come . . ." (Gal. 4:4)

For God, all things exist in an eternal present, without past and future. Time and years for Scripture are certain moments for a new undertaking within the unique history of the world "(Cf. Jn.2,4;7,7,30;13,1)."

As Lord of history, God determines the times and the years, the seasons, and the significant stations in the historical process. The Incarnation and the redemption, which is the most important time in the history of mankind, took place when the proper time had come as God had determined in the eternal plan of salvation. When mankind was prepared to come to faith, when humanity was ready to receive a spiritually higher truth (cf. 1 Tim. 2:6; Tit. 1:3), then "God sent forth his Son, born of woman, born under the law, to redeem those who were under the law, so that we might receive adoption as sons"(Gal. 4:4-5). Here the Apostles are speaking of the Incarnation of God, not of the divinization of man.

Born of Woman... Born of the Holy Spirit and Mary the Virgin.

Sin and the fall came from woman, and from a woman also came salvation and elevation. In the beginning, God the Logos took earth from the ground, clay to form man in the image and likeness of God. Now at the Incarnation, God the Logos took from the Virgin Mary fallen human nature, to reform it in Himself, to make it a new creation, a new world. The sin of man brought corruption and death into the world. And the creator Logos took on human nature to refashion it and to give us incorruptibility by grace; to attack and to overcome sin, corruption, and death, using His human nature, and in Himself to restore human nature to its original status of glory, in communion with God the creator.

In the icon of "Platytera," we can see depicted in a most lively manner the idea of the Incarnation. Christ received human flesh, glorified it in Himself, and raised it to heaven.

That We Might Receive Adoption as Sons...

Man was created to live in communion with God, with a relationship to God as a son to a Father, a relationship of love and freedom. The boast of the Jews was that they were sons of God; that they were not orphans and strangers, far from God (cf. Mk. 7:27-28; Mt. 17:26). With sin man lost this relationship with God; he became a slave to the world, to passions, to his weaknesses. Man came under the curse of the Law. He does not do

B. THE MYSTERY OF THE DIVINE PLAN OF SALVATION IN CHRIST

the good by nature, but by the demand of the law. Christ came to liberate us from sin and the Law, to bring us back to the Father, where we find the first blessedness of our relationship with God and delight in the joy of adoption. The sonship of man and the fatherhood of God is the main theme of the Gospel. Christ is the only Son of God, and we, united with Christ, become beloved children of God (Jn. 1:12; Rom. 8:14-17; Gal. 4:4-7). The Son of God became the Son of Man so that man might become a son of God, a Theanthropos by grace. This is what the Apostles taught us, and this is how the Church interpreted and defined the doctrines. Christ is called and is truly Theanthropos-God-Man: Perfect God and perfect Man. This is the doctrinal formulation of the Fourth Ecumenical Council: "Perfect in His divinity and perfect in His humanity; of the same essence as the Father in His divinity, and of the same essence as we are in His humanity. There is only one and the same Christ... who is known in two natures that are unconfused, unchanged, indivisible, and inseparable. Christ is not separated in two persons... for He is the one and the very same begotten Son, God the Logos and Lord Jesus Christ." In the hypostatic union, the divine nature did not suffer change, nor was the human nature lost in the infinite divinity of the Logos. Both natures in Christ kept their proper characteristics even after the union.

The Fathers did not formulate the doctrines with human syllogisms, but rather with the mind of Sacred Scripture and the Tradition of the Church. They do not speak about the essence of the Logos in His eternal existence, but rather they speak about the Incarnation that took place in the divine plan for the salvation of the world. Both the Apostles and the Fathers emphasized the union of the two natures in Christ, first because only through union with Christ can man be saved, and second because they wished to protect the truth of the Gospel from the dangers of heresy.

Salvation as a Healing Process.

The Apostles and the Fathers of the Church have experienced our salvation in Christ as a spiritual healing and renewal of humanity by the real unity of divine and human nature in the Person of Christ. "What is not assumed remains unhealed, is not restored. What is united to God is restored to its original beauty"(Gregory the Theologian, Letter 101). The human nature assumed by Christ and united with His divine nature has been healed, sanctified, and deified. Now every man through a mystical union with Christ can be healed, forgiven, and saved. Man can be sanctified to the extent that he allows Christ to live in him, and himself to live a life of faith, worship, and love (Gal. 2:20; Rom. 8:3-17).

Christ came to heal in Himself the fallen human nature, and through humanity to regenerate the whole world (Rom. 8:18-23).

Therefore, in Christ, there is a real union of two natures, two wills, and two energies, but one Person. We worship the God-Man as one Person. We do not worship creation, but the Creator who received the created body. The Creator Logos

B. THE MYSTERY OF THE DIVINE PLAN OF SALVATION IN CHRIST

took on creation to refashion it and to recapitulate the whole world in Himself. In the Person of Christ, we have a new creation and union of all. In the mystical union with Christ, everyone and everything finds the unity and perfection that were lost because of sin (Eph. 1:10, 22-23; Col. 1:16-20).

The union of the two natures in Christ is for eternity indivisible and inseparable. Christ is God-Man forever. As God-Man now He can sit at the throne, at the right hand of the Father, and still be with us in Spirit "to the close of the age." He will be our King and Archpriest until all things will be subjected to Him, and through Him to God, "that God may be everything to everyone" (1 Cor. 15:24-28). He will be our King unto the ages of ages (Rev. 22:5), for this is the end goal of the world of God.

This recapitulation of all in Christ is the vision of the unified history of the world according to Sacred Scriptures. God the Father creates and recreates the world through the Son and Logos in the Holy Spirit (Jn. 1:3, 3:16; 1 Cor. 8:6: Heb. 1:2-4).

C. OUR SALVATION THROUGH THE PASSION OF CHRIST

1. *The Cross of Christ*

Another difficult aspect in the divine plan of salvation is the Cross. Salvation had to come about with the Passion of Christ the Savior upon the Cross. The sacrifice of Christ on the Cross is at the center and the heart of the Christian faith. The Gospel is the gospel of the Cross. St. Paul preaches nothing but "Christ crucified… the power of God and the wisdom of God" unto salvation (1 Cor. 1:23, 2:2). The only boast of St. Paul is "in the cross of our Lord Jesus Christ" (Gal. 6:14). The work of salvation was accomplished upon the Cross; it is there that Christ said, "It is finished." The Church now lives with faith in the sacrifice of Christ on the Cross. It is remarkable that the Evangelists dedicate such a large portion of their gospels to describe the sacrifice of Christ on the Cross. The Cross became the symbol of our salvation from the very beginning of the Church.

Why the Cross?

The mind of man stands still before the prayer of Christ in Gethsemane: "My Father, if it be possible, let this cup pass from me..."(Mt. 26:39; Lk. 22:42-44). Even more so is the mind of man stunned with the prayer upon the Cross itself: "My God, my God, why hast thou forsaken me?" (Ps. 22:1 Man asks himself: Why the Cross? Why this cruel death for the salvation of the world? The Evangelists present the events simply, without attempting to interpret them. When the Evangelists were writing the gospels, the Church was living by faith in the saving power of the Cross (Gal. 2:15-21). Why the Cross? An easy response to the question would be that people do not love a righteous man. Christ the righteous came into the world and the people of this world did not accept Him because He taught and lived the truth without compromise and because He said: "I am the Son of God." One disciple from among the twelve betrayed Him, and the people crucified Him with the help of their enemies, the Romans (Jn. 1:10-11; Wis. Sol. 2:10-25).

"It is Written."

The only thing that faith can say about the mystery of the Cross is the fact that "it is written." It is written in Sacred Scripture. Therefore, this too belongs to the eternal plan of God. It

C. OUR SALVATION THROUGH THE PASSION OF CHRIST

is in this: "It is written," in this deep plunge into the eternal will of God, that all the questions that haunt us receive an answer and are illumined. God knew from the beginning of the fall of man, that, out of love for man, He had determined in His eternal plan of salvation even the Passion of the Messiah-Savior, His Son. Scripture had said as much from the beginning (Gen. 3:15). This is how the Prophets saw the Messiah, as the Son-Servant of God who suffers for mankind (Is. 53:1-12; Heb. 2:14-18). Thus Christ foreknew what would happen to Him and He foretold it to His disciples (Mk. 8:27-33). And this is how He interpreted the event after the Resurrection. The Cross was the eternal will of God. And this is why Christ said, "Father, thy will be done" (Lk. 22:42; 24:25-27).

The Cross as a Ransom for Redemption

Sacred Scripture, using the contemporary language of slavery, presents The Cross as a ransom. For a slave to be freed a ransom had to be paid to the owner. Christ came "to give his life as a ransom for many," to "lay down his life for his friends" (Mk. 10:45; Jn. 15:13). But the question remains: To whom was the ransom paid? Some said to God, in order to forgive us. But God has always loved man, and it is He Himself who gave His Son for our salvation (Jn. 3:16). Others said to the devil. But the devil does not own anybody, and God can never pay a ransom to the devil!

The Cross and the Righteousness of God

In Rom. 3:25 St. Paul, the student of the Mosaic Law, says that the sacrifice of Christ on the Cross was made to show the righteousness of God. Righteousness is a major theme in the teaching of St. Paul, and it has a great deal to do with salvation and the inheritance of the kingdom of God. Only God is righteous in His actions, judgments, and promises. After God, the Messiah is also righteous, who brings righteousness in the world. Finally, the man of God is righteous, too, the man who lives a life according to the will of God, who believes in God, and observes all the commandments of God. But truly righteous is the man who will indeed appear righteous before the eyes of God, the one whom God will justify and recognize as righteous. This righteous man will be saved, will have life, and will inherit the glory of the kingdom of God. Thus the righteousness of God means justification and redemption. In reality, however, no one observes all the commandments. "None is righteous, no, not one." All have sinned and are deprived of the glory which God gives. And certainly, no one is saved by his works alone (Rom. 3:9-20).

But God has not always punished sin, and this may be considered as an injustice in God, as tolerance of sin. This is why in the sacrifice of Christ, St. Paul does not only see the love of God, but also the justice of God. It is in the sacrifice of Christ that we learn that God is always just. Sometimes it seems that God has overlooked sin. This is so because from the beginning of the

C. OUR SALVATION THROUGH THE PASSION OF CHRIST

world God, who had foreseen the fall of man, had foreordained Christ, the Messiah-Savior to be given as a ransom, as an expiation for the forgiveness and liberation of mankind from the slavery of sin and death, and as a means of regeneration and perfection of the world in Him. This is the very depth of the mystery of Christ. In the sacrifice of Christ on the Cross, we see how much the righteous God hates sin, but also how much He loves man. As God, He knows that free man will sin, but as a good and loving God, He has also foreseen the means of saving man freely in Christ. God for this reason sent His righteous Son at the proper time to become man and to sacrifice Himself for the salvation of all mankind. Christ, the only righteous one, brings righteousness and salvation to the world. "Since all have sinned and fall short of the glory of God, they are justified by his grace as a gift, through the redemption which is in Christ Jesus, whom God put forward as an expiation by his blood, to be received by faith. This was to show God's righteousness because in his divine forbearance he had passed over former sins; it was to prove at the present time that he himself is righteous and that he justifies him who has faith in Jesus" (Rom. 3:23-26; Jn. 3:16; Eph. 2:6-8; 1 Tim. 2:5-6). Thus all the sacrifices of the Old Testament were representative. They were all types and shadows of the one sacrifice of Christ (Heb. 8:5; 10:1-14). The sacrifice of Christ is the fulfillment of all the sacrifices. Christ died for us and instead of us. He died as our representative, in our place; He died the death which all of us should have died for our sins, for the wages of sin is death.

Truly, then, the Cross is a representative and a salutary sacrifice. Men sinned and were under the curse and the wrath of God, subject to the punishment of death. To be released from this punishment, someone righteous and free from the verdict of death had to give himself as ransom to liberate humanity from the slavery of sin and death. Christ "died for sins once for all, the righteous for the unrighteous, that he might bring us to God" (1 Pet. 3:18).

The sacrifice of Christ is the only sacrifice the Church has to offer to God and she lives by mystically sharing in it until He comes again (1 Cor. 11:23-26).

The Cross is the Righteousness and Love of God

This is what St. Paul has told us, and it is with this truth that the Church lives. These thoughts about the Cross of Christ are human thoughts expressed in the language of faith of that time. But the reality of the Cross will always remain an inapproachable and inscrutable mystery for the mind of man. Only to the extent that it is revealed to great men of faith will we also be able to approach this mystery, and even then we will only be able to approach it as "in a mirror dimly" (1 Cor. 13:12).

The main thing that all of us see and understand in the mystery is the great love of God for man. In the sacrificial death of Christ on the Cross, we have the synthesis of the righteousness and the love of God. As righteous, God hates and punishes sin. "The wages of sin is death" (Rom. 6:23). Man sinned and died; he was separated from God. But God

C. OUR SALVATION THROUGH THE PASSION OF CHRIST

who loves mankind and "desires all men to be saved," has indeed saved them in His Son. In the Person of Christ, God bent down and became man out of love for humanity. He took upon Himself our sins; He became Himself sin and died upon the Cross so that men may become righteous, holy, and be saved freely, by grace through faith in Christ. This then is the righteousness of God that was revealed in Christ. In contrast to the righteousness of the law, of works, God justifies, makes someone who is impious, weak, and imperfect, into a righteous person, as soon as he comes to believe in the salutary sacrifice of Christ; as soon as he accepts the love of God in Christ, and recognizes Christ as his Lord and Savior. God wants to save His people by His grace, for man cannot be saved by his work alone. Those who want to be justified by the works of the Law "are severed from Christ, are fallen away from grace;" they become slaves of the Law (Gal. 2:15-21, 5:1-4). This is why faith is emphasized as the unique and necessary means for salvation.

The Cross is God's Last Invitation for Faith

Faith is what God wants from His people, not our imperfect deeds, although there is no faith without works. Faith is something deeper and broader than deeds. In faith we recognize our God as Father; we give our heart to Him and live a life with a personal feeling of belonging to God and living in a loving child-father relationship. This is real salvation, our daily communion with God.

The whole "Christ Event," Incarnation, Crucifixion, Resurrection, is a unique movement of God; it is an impassioned invitation of God to His people to come back to Him, to believe in God, to repent, to be forgiven and saved. Christ is the way to the Father. God does not command, He only invites us to come freely, as children and friends, to share His love, to partake in the great banquet of the marriage feast of His Son (Mt. 22:2; Rev. 19:10). Christ, the love of God, came to find the lost sheep and to bring it safely back to the Father (Lk. 15:3-10; 19:10). The story of the prodigal son vividly describes the Father waiting for our return, ready to kill the fatted calf, to celebrate our return to God. And this is what we live in our holy Eucharist.

True faith is our free, sincere answer to this call of God in Christ. The people who answer the divine invitation believe in Christ and commit themselves to the will of God; they place themselves within the mystery of the divine plan of salvation in Christ, and then work for the cause of Christ, for the fulfillment of the kingdom of God, which was prepared for us before the foundation of the world. The world was created to become the kingdom of God (Mt. 25:34), and it is indeed built up by Christ, the God-Man King, as well as by the cooperation of all men of faith. We are all fellow workers of God (1 Cor. 3:9-15).

C. OUR SALVATION THROUGH THE PASSION OF CHRIST

Why the Cross?

The Cross is the mysterious way of God in working out our salvation. In the Cross, we have learned that God is righteous and that He loves the world (Jn. 3:16). In the Cross of love, we have learned that the only way to victory in our life is the way of sacrificial love, which means to follow Christ. The kingdom of God is built on earth through the Cross of our Lord, in cooperation with our own little crosses of loving sacrifice.

This, then, is the meaning of the Cross, the saving love of God in Christ. Christ is the sacrificial love of God that calls us to repentance, faith, and love. Those who really feel this are of God; they believe in Christ and begin the revolution to change the world; they begin to build the kingdom of God on earth as it is in heaven.

Let us know the Christ of the Church. Let us know the meaning of the Cross for our personal life. Let us love one another sacrificially, for life is a loving relationship, and life without God and love is "a life moving toward death."

God the Father Accepted the Sacrifice of Christ

In every sacrifice, man offers something valuable and God accepts the offering and forgives and blesses the one who offers and those for whom he offers the sacrifice. Christ the God-Man, out of love, offered Himself as sacrifice for all of mankind. It is for us that He said upon the Cross: "Father, forgive them this sin" (Lk. 23:34; Jn. 17:17-19).

God accepted this sacrifice and forgives all with the understanding that those forgiven believe in this sacrifice of love and hold Christ as Savior, Lord, and God. Thus the work of salvation in Christ is a work of God: God the Father, out of love for mankind, offered the Son, and the Son is both God and Man. The work of salvation is a recreative work of the loving God, and not at all a matter of satisfying the divine righteousness. To say that God accepted the sacrifice is to say that the work of God in Christ achieved its purpose, its goal. With the Incarnation, the love and the obedience of Christ, the whole of mankind, united with Christ, was forgiven, reconciled, and sanctified. With Christ as the yeast the whole world became a New Creation. Man found his ancient blessedness near God, and with the help of the Holy Spirit, he can live a life in God here and inherit the glory of the Kingdom of God in eternity.

2. *Our Salvation in Christ*

As we said earlier, Christology is also Soteriology, that is, the doctrine of Christ is also the doctrine of salvation. This means that Christ is not just a teacher, He is also our Savior. With His love and obedience unto death on the Cross, Christ delivered us from sin and reconciled us with God. He has restored the distorted image of God in us. He has made us children of God, fellow heirs of the kingdom of God with Himself. Finally, He has done away with death and has granted

C. OUR SALVATION THROUGH THE PASSION OF CHRIST

us the gift of incorruptibility. "We condemned Christ to death, and He condemned us to immortality. Sin brought unnatural corruption, and the creator Logos gave us, by grace, immortality again."

Are We Saved?

Many things have been said about our salvation in Christ through faith. Are we already saved, or are we being saved in Christ? The truth is that Christ died on the Cross for the salvation of us all. With His obedience unto death on the Cross, He delivered us from sin and reconciled us with God. Sin brought with it unnatural corruption and the Creator-Logos, by grace, gave us immortality again. Everyone who believes and is baptized in Christ and in the name of the Holy Trinity is saved, for he has died to the old man and has risen to a newness of life; he has entered the kingdom of God, the realm of the love of God. This salvation, however, is nascent, as St. Paul would say, and like a newborn child, it needs to grow and mature into a perfect man (Eph. 4:13-15) and reach holiness. We are indeed saved and we are continuously being saved in Christ because we are weak and continue to fall. We have inherited the inclination toward sin. But we have been freed by Christ to fight for our sanctification. If we were like St. Paul and St. John we could easily say, "I am saved." St. Paul knew that he had been saved in Christ, but he also knew that the saved believer is still weak and must struggle in his life to stand firmly and conquer the world before he can receive the crown of victory, the final salvation and true adoption (Rom. 8:23-25; Rev. 3:5; Phil. 2:5-12; 3:12; 2 Tim. 4:8).

Believing that "I am saved" is a psychological assurance which encourages men to live a life in Christ. "I am being saved" is a warning not to relax in our fight. Salvation is regeneration and this is a life-long process. We know we are holy in Christ, yet we must continuously sanctify ourselves till we reach the likeness of Christ in our life. We are being saved by Christ because we are weak, but only through our cooperation with the divine grace. There is no magic salvation by empty faith. Life is a spiritual race. We are soldiers and athletes of Christ fighting for the final goal.

Everything in the world is imperfect. The formless matter needs to reach its form, to become cosmos, as Plato and Aristotle would have said. We are destined to be "conformed to the image" of the Son of God.

Our life then is a journey to salvation in Christ. Christ Himself is still in agony over us, and the salutary energy of the Cross continues in the Church until He comes again. We may sin even now, but we have Christ who forgives us. Sin is the only enemy that separates us from God. Yet Christ is always there as our representative, the Lamb slain and interceding for our forgiveness. God sees Christ in every one of us. And no sin is greater than the love of God in Christ (1 Jn. 2:1-2; Rom. 8:39). We need to repent, to ask for forgiveness, and to make a new start.

C. OUR SALVATION THROUGH THE PASSION OF CHRIST

Grace, Faith, and Works

Salvation is indeed the work and gift of divine grace. But grace needs the cooperation of the will of man. Our works are not meritorious; we cannot earn our salvation by our works only, for they are imperfect. But nonetheless, they are necessary for our salvation. Grace, faith, and works go together. Without works faith is dead, and a dead faith does not save. Without living faith, man is weak and cannot do any good works (Jn. 15:5; Phil. 4:13).

Divine grace is continuously changing our hearts and strengthening our minds and our wills so that we can say "No" to sin and "Yes" to the good, as we come to know God and see His glory and His grace in us and around us. In the final analysis, we must say that man is saved as long as he remains in Christ, fighting the good fight together with Him.

The Adam-Christ Relationship and the Salvation of Mankind (Rom. 5:12-19; 1 Cor. 15:22, 45-55)

Our faith tells us that the whole of humanity has been saved in the Person of Christ. The whole of humanity is one and unified, with one purpose and one plan of God for its salvation. The human race began with Adam, the first man, and it proceeds toward its goal. Adam is the first head of the human race. All human beings come from Adam. We could even say that the whole human race pre-existed in Adam. Christ came at a certain time in history to help us to reach our final goal; to become the kingdom of God, a community of people living in faith and love and in perfect personal communion with God the creator.

According to St. Paul, Christ is not simply a historical person, a prophet, or a teacher, not even the greatest of these in the world. St. Paul sees a deeper relationship between Christ and mankind. As man, Christ is the second Adam or the final Adam, and He constitutes a special station in the history of unified humanity. All believers belong to Him as their Savior and Lord. They live in Him and are one body with Christ, their Head. Adam and Christ are two successive heads or leaders of the human race. They are indeed different and have caused different results for all humanity.

Adam, the first man, was created as a copy, "a type of the one who is to come" in the future. Adam awaits his antitype, the final Adam, Jesus Christ (Rom. 5:12-18). Christ is the antitype of Adam; Christ is the perfect Man, the true image of God the Father. In Christ, we have the perfection of man. Christ is the "idea" of man, as Plato would say. And the goal of man as an individual person or as humanity is to become Christ-like; to be conformed to the image of Christ (Rom. 8:29).

St. Paul describes the relationship of Adam and Christ. In Adam and Christ, we have two types or patterns of man. Adam is the first man, the head of humanity; he was created from the earth and is earthly. He is corruptible and mortal. All created

C. OUR SALVATION THROUGH THE PASSION OF CHRIST

beings are mortal. The second man, Christ, came from heaven and is heavenly, incorruptible, and immortal. Adam became a living being, capable of living the natural life. The final Adam, that is, Christ, became a life-giving Spirit. Especially after the Resurrection, Christ gives the Holy Spirit who in turn gives life to the faithful (Jn. 3:16; 10:10; 20:22), rebuilds the old man, and makes him a new creation in Christ (2 Cor. 5:17). "As was the man of dust, so are those who are of the dust; and as is the man of heaven, so are those who are of heaven" (1 Cor. 15:48). In Christ indeed we have seen a body and a life of a supernatural form, especially as we have seen Christ in His Transfiguration and His appearances after the Resurrection and at the Ascension. And this is how St. Paul saw Christ as the Lord of (1 Cor. 2:8; Acts 1:9; 9:3). Now, we, as inheritors of both Adam and Christ, have to copy them. This is the successive relation of Adam and Christ, realized in the development of man as humanity and as individual persons. This was in the plan of God for humanity from the beginning. We had to grow from a lower level of physical life to a higher spiritual level of life. "It is not the spiritual which is first but the physical, and then the spiritual" (1 Cor. 15:45- 46).

Now we inherit both physical and spiritual life. As in Adam, we inherited the natural man with his corruption and death, so now we inherit from Christ incorruptibility and immortality. Our life is a spiritual struggle to renew ourselves in the Holy Spirit; to put on Christ, the new Man. This struggle must continue in us until all that "is mortal in us may be swallowed by life." "For this perishable nature must put on the imperishable, and this mortal nature must put on immortality." Finally, there will be victory over death and over sin which leads to death. "But thanks be to God who gives us the victory..." The grace and the glory belong to God who gave us the victory through our Lord Jesus Christ (1 Cor. 15:42-57; 2 Cor. 5:2-4; Rom. 5:12-21).

Humanity, as we have already noted, is one, unified and continuous, according to the Fathers. In the flesh which Christ received, the whole of human nature is present as it was in Adam. The whole of humanity is contained in the Person of Christ as the new spiritual genarch. We are all thus one body with Christ as our head. Sacred Scripture sees all things in one unity within eternity, from the creation of Adam, the Incarnation, the Resurrection of Christ, and up to our own resurrection.

If we apply the idea of the unity of humanity to the mystery of Christ, we can say this: In the sacrifice of Christ on the Cross all of us were co-crucified with Christ; we have all repented and have been forgiven. The victory of Christ over sin is ours; Christ won the battle for us. But we are continuously repenting and being co-crucified and saved in Christ. In Baptism we are co-crucified and share the death of Christ. In the holy Eucharist, we are co-offering ourselves as sacrifice together with Christ. In our everyday life we are fighting against evil powers (Eph. 6:1-18; Rev. 9:16). The question, however, is to what ex-

C. OUR SALVATION THROUGH THE PASSION OF CHRIST

tent we truly repent and are committed to and co-crucified with Christ, walking in newness of life, in order to build together the kingdom of God (Rom. 6:1-6; Gal. 2:19-20; Eph. 4:22-24).

Our Salvation is Spiritual Transformation

Flesh and blood cannot inherit the kingdom of God, nor can the perishable inherit the imperishable (1 Cor. 15:50). The physical man, as he came from Adam, is mortal and mortality has no place in the glorious life of eternity. Therefore, we need to change, to be spiritually transformed. We have to put on our "wedding garment" to enter the marriage feast of our Lord, to enter the kingdom of God. "As we have borne the image of the man of dust (Adam), we shall also bear the image of the man of heaven." This spiritual transformation starts in our life here and now. Now we must put off the old man with his practices and desires, and put on the new man in Christ. We have to put on Christ (Gal. 3:27). We must let the new life in Christ swallow up the mortal within us, so that we may say with St. Paul: "I have been crucified with Christ; it is no longer I who live, but Christ who lives in me; and the life I now live in the flesh I live by faith in the Son of God, who loved me and gave himself for me" (Gal. 2:20). This means that our salvation is a transformation in Christ, as a spiritual sharing in the redemptive sacrifice of Christ and in His Resurrection. Our perfect transformation will take place in our own resurrection, as an act and gift of God in Christ (Rom. 6:3-6, 8-11; 1 Cor. 15:22, 42-43, 51-52; Phil. 321).

The Mystical Vision of the End

St. Paul envisions the end as a series of events at the general resurrection as if enacted before his own eyes. "Lo, I tell you a mystery... we shall all be changed... at the last trumpet... the dead will be raised imperishable and we (who are still living at that moment) shall be changed... When the perishable puts on imperishable, and the mortal will put on immortality, then shall come to pass the saying that is written: Death is swallowed up in victory. O death where is thy victory? O death where is thy sting?" (1 Cor. 15:51-55). There St. Paul sees the eternal hope of man, the abolition of death, the last enemy of man and of the kingdom of God. This is the greatest contribution of the Evangelion, the Good News to man from God in Christ, namely, freedom from the fear of death. Death is indeed the ultimate enemy of man and it covers everything with darkness. The weapon of death is the poisoning sting of sin. And sin in turn is strengthened by the Mosaic Law or any external law. The law is a witness to sin, but it cannot help man to avoid sin. Thus, man was a slave to sin, captured as a slave under the law, subject to death, and under the wrath and sentence of God. But we are finally free from all of these evils by the love of God in our Lord Jesus Christ. Christ has freed us from sin, from the condemnation of the law, and from the fear of death. This is the main message of the Christian faith. This is why St. Paul finally exclaims joyfully, first in thanksgiving and then in exhortation: "Thanks be to God, who gives us the victory

C. OUR SALVATION THROUGH THE PASSION OF CHRIST

through our Lord Jesus Christ. Therefore, my beloved brethren, be steadfast, immovable, always abounding in the work of the Lord, knowing that in the Lord your labor is not in vain" (1 Cor. 15:51-58).

The First-Born of All Creation (Col. 1:15-23)

Another important term that creates misunderstandings about the Person of Christ is the term "first-born." The first-born is the first son of a family, without necessarily requiring that there be other sons after the first.

The first-born had special rights in the family. He was the first to inherit the rights of the father. The title of first-born has also been used in other ways. Israel is the "first-born of God," because it is the elect and beloved people of God. The king of Israel is also first-born. The title belonged particularly to the expected Messiah-Savior (Gen. 25:31-34; Ex. 4:22; Ps. 88/89:27). First-born is also a title attributed to Christ as the first-born of the Virgin Mary. The title first-born for Christ does not mean that other sons followed His birth. Rather, it signifies the important position and mission that He holds in the world as Savior and King (Cf. Lk. 1:32-33, 2:7-11). For the New Testament Christ is the only begotten Son of God; He cannot have other brothers. The so-called brothers of Christ might have been children of Joseph through a previous wife, or they might have been relatives. Scripture sometimes refers to relatives as brothers. First-born is a title of honor, especially for elect people, and Christ is the "elect of God," "his Chosen

One" (Lk. 23:35; cf. Gen. 31:46-54). St. Paul uses the term to emphasize the close relationship between Christ and humanity in salvation.

In the New Testament Christ is the first-born of God in a particular sense as the Son of God (Heb. 1:2-8). Christ is called "the first-born of all creation," and this indicates clearly that the title does not apply to His relationship with other brothers, but to His unique place in the world as leader, king, savior, and giver of life. Christ is first-born, not first-created among other creatures. Christ is begotten of the Father and exists "before all," before the creation of the world. He is not a creature, but the creator of all created things. He is the first-born, the leader of the world because "all things were created in Him, by Him and for Him." All things, the earthly and the heavenly, have been created by Christ. In Him, they have their being and in Him, they are held together in existence and unity. Thus the believing Church sees the whole world in Christ. Life itself began with Christ and all things have existence in Him, and all things move toward Christ as the final goal. And our goal is one: to become Christ-like, to be conformed to the image of the Son of God, to become the kingdom of God with Christ as the eternal King, to become "the first born who are enrolled in heaven" (Col. 1:15-17; 2:11; Rom. 8:29; 11:33-36; 1 Cor. 15:24-28; Rev. 22:5; Heb. 12:23).

C. OUR SALVATION THROUGH THE PASSION OF CHRIST

Christ the First Fruit

The Jews offered their first fruits as a thanksgiving to God. Christ is the first who offered Himself as a sacrifice to God and thus became the ἀπαρχή, that is, the first fruits of faith, obedience, and love for God the Father. Even the first Christians were called the first fruits, the elect. But Christ offered Himself as king, high priest, and shepherd on behalf of His people. And we who believe and follow, who suffer with and are co-crucified with Christ, are also the "first fruits," the select first harvest offered to God and to Christ (Rev. 14:4: Jam. 1:18).

Christ the First-Born of the Dead

God accepted the offering and raised Christ, as the first fruit, or the first-born from the dead, the first flower of the new life of the resurrection. The first fruits however will eventually bring about also the full harvest, the general resurrection at the time of His Parousia (1 Cor. 15:21-28, 50-58; Col. 1:18). St. Paul himself, who meditated deeply on all these matters, did not wait for the general resurrection; he lived the new life in Christ here and now, and saw everything as being present and fulfilled. God called us and justified us, and in Christ who rose from the dead, He has already glorified us (Rom. 8:28-30; Col. 1:13). And Christ as the first-born of all creation and the first-born of the dead will also be the first-born of all in the new life of the Resurrection.

3. Christ and the Church (Col. 1:18-23)
Christ is the Head of the Body, the Church

If Christ is the head, the creator, and the purpose of the world, He is particularly the creator, the head, and the first-born of the Church, the first-born among many brothers in the new life of the Resurrection (Rom. 8:29). Christ is the first-born from the dead, the first who escaped from the realm of the dead and created the Church, the kingdom of the new humanity. The Church is a new creation built on the Resurrection of Christ. If anyone is in Christ, he is a new creation (2 Cor. 5:17). Thus, Christ, the God-Man is the first-born of all creation, the first-born of many brethren, the head of the Church. He is preeminent in everything, because "in him dwells the whole fullness of deity bodily" (Col. 1:15-20, 2:9).

The Church is the place where our Lord continues His Lordship for the salvation of the world (Jn. 17:2) until all the world is saved, becomes "cosmos," kingdom of God, people of God (1 Tim. 2:4). The Church is the redeemed people of God and must be one. The Church is Christ Himself and Christ cannot be divided. Differences of opinion will exist, for we are human beings. Yet our differences must be solved by faith and love in the Holy Spirit. This was the way of the Church of the first nine centuries. The result of this unity of the Church constitutes the treasures of Sacred Tradition: unity of faith in God, in the divine plan of salvation, in the Person of Christ, in the life of the Church.

C. OUR SALVATION THROUGH THE PASSION OF CHRIST

Without these treasures of Sacred Tradition, we cannot speak about Christian faith. We speak only of philosophical systems according to human traditions and not according to Christ (Col. 1:8-10). Thus we do not build up the Church of Christ.

The Church was built upon the Resurrection of Christ (Mt. 28:18-20; Rom. 1:4). As Theanthropos the risen Christ has reconciled the world to God, and the work of reconciliation and sanctification is continuing in the Church (2 Cor. 5:17-21) until He shall come again. Christ and the Church are connected inseparably and have a universal significance. Christ identifies Himself with the Church (Acts 9:4-5; Rom. 12:4-5; 1 Cor. 12:12).

He Humbled Himself (Phil. 2:5-11)

A problem which troubled St. Paul in his apostolic work was the sin of pride. It was pride which ate away at the Jewish people, and it is pride which is now disturbing the Christian churches, creating quarrels and schisms. For this reason, St. Paul strongly emphasized the need for humility in the preservation of the unity of the Church: "Do nothing from selfishness or conceit, but in humility count others better than yourselves." "Put on... lowliness, meekness." "Do not be haughty, but associate with the lowly; never be conceited"(Phil. 2:3; Col. 3:12; Rom. 12:10-16; 1 Cor. 3:3).

Writing very personally to his beloved Church in Philippi, St. Paul beseeched the faithful to live with love, humility, and concord among themselves in order to maintain unbroken the unity of the Church which is always in danger of being broken by the egotism and the vanity of certain persons (1:27; 2:1-4). Out of a similar concern, St. Paul wrote the magnificent hymn to love (1 Cor. 13).

"Have this mind among yourselves, which you have in Christ Jesus." In your relationships you have to think and to live as Christ Himself thought and lived. All of the faith and the life of Christians must be determined from above, as we have seen and received them in the Person of Christ. There we find all the laws and the regulations of the moral, the social, and the religious life. This is why Christ became man so that we might have Him as the example in our life. In the Person of Christ, we have seen how God works for the salvation of the world, with love to the point of self-sacrifice, with obedience and humility. And service to mankind in love and humility is the way to achieve our high goals.

In the exceptional passage of the Letter to the Philippians (2:5- 11), St. Paul presents in a passionate way the Person of Christ as the heavenly prototype of humility, which the Church must always take seriously into account if it is to bear worthily His name. He presents to us poetically and dogmatically his teaching about God, Christ, and the Church.

C. OUR SALVATION THROUGH THE PASSION OF CHRIST

"Though He Was in the Form of God"

Christ for St. Paul is an eternal Person. Before the Incarnation, during the Incarnation, and after the Resurrection, Christ was and is unto eternity "in the form of God", that is, of the same nature and honor and glory as the Father; He has "equality with God." This equality with God was not considered by Christ as "a thing to be grasped," as something that one acquires by force and zealously holds on to, never to let go, for He was by nature the Son of God and equal to the Father. Thus He did not hold on to this position of equality with God exclusively for Himself, "but emptied himself, taking the form of a servant." Christ relinquished for a period of time His place of honor and came and took the place of a servant. This is the great self-emptying of the Son: He who was in the form of God took on the form of a servant. He was born in the likeness of man, He became man, in order to help man come to be in the likeness of God, which was, after all, his destiny from creation.

St. Paul sees Christ, the Son of God, eternally in the form of God, while St. John sees Him as the divine Logos. But both see the Incarnation taking place in time for the salvation of the world. They are freely expressing their established faith in Christ (cf. Heb. 1:2-4).

"And Being Found in Human Form He Humbled Himself and Became Obedient unto Death."

As man, Christ was obedient to the will of the Father for the salvation of the world, even though as Son He had the same will as the Father. In obedience to the will of the Father, Christ took upon Himself the sins of all of us; He took our sinful place and died as the ultimate sinner. He died the most cruel and humiliating death on the Cross. He died the death which all of us should have died for our sin. With His love and the obedience unto death to the will of God, Christ overcame the power of sin and of death. He tore up the paper containing our sins and accusations and nailed it to the Cross as invalid. He tore down the middle wall of enmity that existed between men and God; He united us among ourselves and with Himself; and as a new God-Man, He reconciled and united us all with God (2 Cor. 5:19-21; Eph. 2:16; Col. 2:14; 1 Pet. 1:24).

The Lordship of Christ Over All

"Therefore God has highly exalted Him and bestowed on Him the name which is above every name... Lord Jesus Christ." (Phil. 2:9) Because Christ humbled Himself and suffered out of love for the salvation of mankind, God exalted Him and made Him Lord of all. The Son, being in the form of God, had His glory near the Father, before the world was created. Now that the Incarnate Christ has completed His work of salvation, the Father has exalted Him and has given Him as a reward-prize

C. OUR SALVATION THROUGH THE PASSION OF CHRIST

the name of Lord. Lord is an authoritative name that is above every name that anyone on earth or heaven can imagine. In the Old Testament the name Lord is the name of God, and the Church, by giving the name Lord to Christ, makes Him equal to God, and attributes to Him "equality with God."

"That at the name of Jesus every knee should bow, in heaven and on earth and under the earth, and every tongue confess that Jesus Christ is Lord, to the glory of God the Father." Christ is the Savior of the world and at His name angels and men, in heaven and on earth, bow their knee in worshipful reverence and confess openly that Jesus Christ is Lord. The main title of Christ is Lord. "The Lord Jesus" or "Jesus is Lord" is the formal confession in the Holy Spirit of the Christians. With this confession of baptism, the faithful declare precisely that they belong to Christ as Savior and Lord of their life (1 Cor. 12:3; Col. 3:7; Rom. 10:9).

"To the Glory of God the Father."

The three Persons of the Holy Trinity are homoousia, of one essence and of equal honor. But because the Father is the first source of divinity, He holds a particular position in the one divinity, and the Fathers of the Church refer to this as the monarchy of the Father.

The purpose of the creation of the world is the glory of God. And the glory of God will be realized fully when the work of salvation through the Lord Jesus Christ is completed; when the whole of mankind, the entire universe believes and confesses Christ as Savior and Lord and is subjected to the will of God (Jn. 17:1-8; 1 Cor. 24- 28).

Are all of these thoughts of St. Paul theology or ethics? They are neither theology nor ethics, but they do shed light on both. There can be no ethics without theology as its basis. St. Paul does not develop a dogmatic theology. He does not speak about the nature of the pre-existent Christ, nor about the manner of the Incarnation. He takes all of them for granted in the faith of the Philippians. The Apostle Paul sees the crucified and resurrected Christ and presents Him to the faithful as the only example of Christian life. But the manner by which he presents Christ to the eyes of the faithful becomes the most vibrant confession of the faith of St. Paul and of the Church. What, after all, is theology, but the faith of the Apostles? According to this faith of St. Paul and of the Church, Christ exists eternally "in the form of God." He did not hold on to the position of glory and equality with God in an egotistical manner. But in time, He "emptied himself," He willingly gave up the position of glory and came and took the position of a servant; He became man similar to us (the very opposite of what the devil advised the forefathers in the Garden of Eden, Gen. 3:4-5). In becoming man, Christ humbled Himself and lived in obedience to the will of God for the salvation of the world. Christ died upon the Cross to save and to raise man up to God. This is why

C. OUR SALVATION THROUGH THE PASSION OF CHRIST

Christ is the Lord and the Savior of the world, and why He is acknowledged and worshiped by angels and men, in heaven and on earth.

The lordship of the Father and the lordship and the glory of the Son is one and the same. And Christ will reign forever with the faithful (Rev. 5:13; 11:15; 22:3), or God will govern His people through Jesus Christ.

This is the insightful plunge which St. Paul made into the mystery of Christ. In the Person of Christ, Paul has seen the mystery of the life of God in His relationship with man. He has seen how God thinks and acts in love to save His people whom He loves so much (Jn. 3:16; Rom. 5:8; 8:32; Gal. 4:4-5). St. Paul went behind the Incarnation to the eternal existence of the Son in the form of God. And then he proceeded beyond the earthly life of Christ and the humility of the Cross to His exaltation and to His universal lordship. St. Paul also proceeded from His presence in the Church, in the Spirit, struggling against the ungodly powers, to the end of the journey of the world, and even beyond that to the eternal glory of God. St. John did the same thing (Jn. 1:1; 17:24-26). But it was St. Paul, however, who approached the Incarnation and the Passion much more closely. It is St. Paul who portrays Christ crucified to the faithful (Gal. 3:1).

This is the faith of St. Paul and it is this faith which changed the persecutor Saul into Paul the Apostle of Christ. This is why St. Paul, writing personally to his beloved Philippians about humility, can so readily present his teaching about the Person and the work of Christ in the precise words and terms that give us a rather complete theology and Christology of the Church. The recipients of the Letter must have known the meaning of the message he wrote, and St. Paul does not see the need to offer additional explanations. In his preaching St. Paul had already depicted Christ crucified before the eyes of the faithful (cf. Gal. 3:1). It is also possible that this passage (Phil. 2:5-11) was a familiar hymn and doxology of the Church expressing the love of God in Christ (cf. Rom. 8:31-39).

These are the things which the Apostles taught us about the Person and work of Christ, and it is with these doctrines that the Church lives. And the work of God in Christ cannot be approached with rational questions such as "how" and "why," which do not lead us anywhere. Christ is approached as God-Man with faith, with our confession and worship in the fellowship of the redeemed Church. Man lives with faith. And for faith to survive and live it must have spiritual nourishment. It needs humility, love, and obedience. And Christ the Theanthropos, the God-Man, will forever be the unique example of life to which all will look, Christians and non-Christians, even if it is an unreachable example for the weak man.

C. OUR SALVATION THROUGH THE PASSION OF CHRIST

4. Sin and the Divine Plan of Salvation

A basic doctrine of Sacred Scripture and of the Church is the existence of sin and the forgiveness of sins through the sacrifice of Christ on the Cross (1 Jn. 1:8-9). We cannot begin to understand the mystery of Christ if we do not understand the destructive power of sin and accept our responsibility for it as free human beings. For it is a great sin indeed to deny the personal responsibility we all have for sin and to regard others responsible for it.

Sin is a free act of free man. It is introduced by free man through the instigation of the devil (Gen. 3:1-7; Wis. Sol. 2:23-24), and it is a negation of the good. All of us have inherited the inclination toward sin. Everyone is subject to sin; "all have sinned" (Rom. 3:23). Sin, either personal or original sin, is behind all the problems of life.

Sin (αμαρτία) in a literal sense, is the failure of a certain purpose, as for example, of happiness, of life. According to the Christian faith, sin is the failure of a person to live honorably and worthily of one's calling, as children of the holy God, and in the likeness of God.

Man was created in the image of God, rational and free, master of himself, independent, and lord of the world. Man's free will is the greatest gift of God to man. Free will is what gives majesty to man within the rest of the world of nature, but it is also man's weak point. Everything depends on how we use our free will. Are we going to cooperate with God and attain to His likeness, or are we going to say no to God and live far from Him in sin? "The fear of the Lord is the beginning of knowledge (wisdom)" (Prov. 1:7). "Know thyself" and "follow God," are two remarkable imperatives which the ancients used to say.

Free man sins. An animal does not sin. And man sins against himself, against his neighbor, and against God. He sins against himself when he does not exercise authority and control over his instincts and passions, and when he neglects what is truly good and virtuous. Such a person sins against himself: he is divided spiritually. He is troubled by his conscience and therefore loses his spiritual peace and serenity; he loses the purpose of life; he loses real happiness.

Man sins against his neighbor by word or act and thus loses communion with his fellow human beings. And man is a social being, who needs to be in social contact with other people. In all instances of sin, and this is the most remarkable thing, man sins against God. "I have sinned against heaven and before you" (Lk. 15:18; Ps. 51:1-6), is what the sinner says. Sin is rebellion against God and His will. In life, everything is arranged according to the will of God. The ancient Stoic philosophers used to say that to live according to nature is to live according to right reason and according to the will of God. Thus every sin in life is an act against the will of God. This is why sin is regarded as a disharmony of life, an action of the soul against nature, a sickness of the soul. The

C. OUR SALVATION THROUGH THE PASSION OF CHRIST

first sin took place in Paradise by the instigation of the serpent. Adam and Eve disobeyed the will of God. Man desired to become independent of God, to become himself God.

The Fall of Man

The Church calls sin "the Fall." With sin, man falls from the high position he holds near God. He loses his spiritual superiority and his natural beauty as an image of God. The image of God in man is darkened and distorted. Man loses the purity and the nobleness of his soul and he hides from God. With sin, men and women lose their self-control and independence, becoming slaves, "slaves of sin" (Rom. 6:17-20; 7:13-25). This is why sin is regarded as a sickness or a pollution of the soul.

Why is There Sin?

Socrates, among the ancient Greeks, maintained that the cause of sin is ignorance. A person has to know "what is good in itself" in order to live honorably. And indeed, only one who has experienced the height of holiness can understand well the terrible abyss of the fall of sin. And certainly, only one who is totally depraved spiritually cannot sense the pain of sin, to repent, and be raised up.

Sin Separates Man From God

As rebellion against God, sin brought its own punishment, death, the separation of man from God. For this is precisely what death is separation from God who is life itself. Adam hid himself in the "jungle;" he could no longer look upon God face to face (Gen. 3:1-10. Rom. 5:12-14). A chasm or a wall of partition is raised between man and God. Man cannot speak to God with boldness, to say "Our Father," and feel like a child of God; he lives like a fugitive in a faraway country. And apart from the grace and love of God, there is no life. The temporary satisfaction of sin will never satisfy our soul. Our soul yearns for Christ, for God, and far from God man simply "is dying of hunger" (Lk. 15:17). Man, separated from God, merely exists as a withered flower in a hostile world, without God, without hope (Eph. 2:12).

In the final analysis, sin, when continued, leads to spiritual death. The person who lives in sin is spiritually dead. Since man is spirit when sin enters into the life of man, he simply dies (Gen. 3:1-10; Rom. 6:17-20; 7:13-25).

This is the power of sin and it is in this power of sin where the deep meaning of the Cross lies. Man lost his communion with God and Christ came to restore it. Man sinned and became a slave to sin; Christ became man and as a big brother liberated us from the slavery of sin and from death. He raised us up to our original glory near God. Out of love, Christ took all of our sins upon Himself and nailed them upon the Cross. He died as the scapegoat of the Old Testament for His people (Lev. 16:19), and "by death, he conquered death and gave life to those in the tombs"(Rom. 8:3-4; Col. 2:12-15).

C. OUR SALVATION THROUGH THE PASSION OF CHRIST

Forgiveness of Sin in Christ

Sin makes man a slave to death. To be free from death the sin of man had to be erased, to be forgiven, and only God can forgive sins, for to God we sin. Therefore, at the proper time God sent His Son to free man from slavery to sin and death (Jn. 3:16. Gal. 4:4-7). Christ, the only sinless Man, died on the Cross on behalf of the whole of humanity. He prayed on the Cross for us all: "Father, forgive them for they know not what they do" (Lk. 23:34). And the Father does forgive us when we realize the destructive power of sin; when we repent and believe in the representative sacrifice of our Lord.

In the representative sacrifice of our Lord, the whole of humanity has repented, has been crucified, and has risen together with our Lord in the newness of life (Rom. 6:3-6; Gal. 5:24; Eph. 4:22-24).

Sin introduced death into the world. The redeeming sacrifice of Christ brought forgiveness, reconciliation, and newness of life. Natural death still exists, but it is the gate by which we enter into eternal life (Jn. 5:24; 11:25).

The ministry of the forgiveness and reconciliation and newness of life is given to the Church, where Christ is working out the salvation of the world. Repentance and forgiveness are the main characteristics of Christian faith (Mt. 16:18-19; Lk. 24:47; Jn. 20:21-23; 2 Cor. 5:19-21).

5. The Resurrection, the Ascension

The Resurrection constitutes the main characteristic of Christian faith, and without faith in the Resurrection, our faith in Christ has no foundation. The Christian Church was born out of the faith in the Resurrection of Jesus Christ. "If Christ has not been raised your faith is futile and you are still in your sins... But in fact Christ has been raised from the dead, the first-fruits of those who have fallen asleep" (1 Cor. 15:14-20). The Resurrection of Christ guarantees our own resurrection and salvation.

The Resurrection of Christ is the greatest miracle in history, which is itself a miracle. It is difficult to believe in the Resurrection, especially when one uses his own mind as the measure of all things, and when one forgets that he is a creature. And yet without the Resurrection of Christ, the whole world remains unfathomable, or at least quite gloomy for the person who seeks some meaning in life. Faith can assert that for a creature of God the miracle is to reach the state of perfection for which one was destined at creation or to reach the destiny of one's creation by virtue of a special intervention of God. God can intervene, for He is the Cause and not the subject of natural law. And Resurrection is the miracle by which mankind can reach its destination.

Death is not a natural thing for man who is created in the image and likeness of God. Having received in himself the breath-spirit of God, man was destined to be like God and to live in communion with God. But sin entered human life and brought

C. OUR SALVATION THROUGH THE PASSION OF CHRIST

corruption and death (Gen. 3:5; Rom. 5:12; 6:23). Death, in turn, entered violently into human life as a consequence of sin. But Christ as Man did not sin, and death has no right to claim Him. Christ is life, and life conquered death and arose (Acts 2:24; 3:15). The Church sings triumphantly: "Christ is risen from the dead! By death He conquered death, and to those in the tombs He gave life!"

One cannot prove the reality of the Resurrection by logic. Faith in the Resurrection is based on the facts of the empty tomb and of the appearances of the risen Lord. It is also based upon the influence it had on the eye-witnesses, the disciples, and Apostles. Christ had to eat something before their very eyes to convince the disciples that He is really the risen Christ (Lk. 24:36-43; Jn. 20:25). The Resurrection changed the character of the Apostles and enabled them to proclaim the Gospel throughout the world, and to build the Church of Christ, who is alive and who enlightens the world till now and to the end of time. The risen Lord is still the light of the world (Jn. 1:5).

For forty days the resurrected Christ appeared to the disciples bodily, but in "another form" (Mk. 16:12), that is, in the resurrected and deified body, and as each person was prepared to see Him. The Resurrection of Christ is not an illusion of the first Christians. The Apostles had their doubts and their questions upon hearing the first announcements of the Resurrection of Christ. They believed, however, because they were convinced by the facts. Some of the disciples doubted at first because the words about resurrection "seemed to them an idle tale, and they did not believe them" (Lk. 24:11; Mt. 28:17). Thomas wanted to see and to touch the resurrected Christ for himself in order to believe in the reality of the Resurrection. He saw Him and made his clear confession of faith in the Person of Christ: "My Lord and my God!" (Jn. 20:28)

With the Resurrection of Christ and His post-resurrection appearances, the faith of the Apostles was confirmed and made steadfast. With the appearance of the resurrected Christ, Saul, the persecutor, became the fervent Apostle Paul. The faith in the Resurrection of Christ was proclaimed to all the new churches. The Apostles preached the event, referred to the empty tomb, and to the appearances of the resurrected Christ as confirmation, without explanations (1 Cor. 15:1-8; Acts 10:40-41). The Resurrection, together with the Cross, became the faith of the Church, and the Evangelists wrote freely about these events, underlying certain points as each one experienced and understood them. Some wrote in general and some wrote in more detail, but all together they present to us the faith of the Church.

The Resurrection is a creative work of God. It is a turning point in the history of the world. The old dispensation ends and a new one starts, and this is the new life of the power of the Resurrection, the life in the Holy Spirit. With the descent of the Holy Spirit, the period of the Church began where we have the change from this present state of things to the state of eternal life that now has been inaugurated.

C. OUR SALVATION THROUGH THE PASSION OF CHRIST

The Ascension (Lk. 24:50-51; Acts. 1:10)

Only St. Luke, the historian, saved for us a description of the event of the Ascension. He presents the facts and the impression they made upon the Apostles without the exact time and place where they occurred. We are now in the time of the Resurrection and the appearances of the risen Lord are not understood as simply natural; they are indeed heavenly, supernatural realities.

For forty days the risen Lord appeared to His disciples in His transformed and deified body, and spoke to them about the kingdom of God. He continued to prepare them that they may bring the Gospel of the kingdom of God to the whole world. On the fortieth day after the Resurrection, Christ led the disciples out of Jerusalem, as far as Bethany, on the Mount of Olives, where He had prayed the night before the Cross. He spoke to them, He blessed them, and while He was blessing them, "as they were looking on, he was lifted up, and a cloud took him out of their sight" (Acts 1:9), and "he parted from them, and was carried up into heaven" (Lk. 24:51).

The angels who appeared to the disciples testified to the Ascension and assured them that the ascended Jesus will come again in the same way, upon the clouds with His wounded, but deified and glorious body. Having seen the Lord in His glory and having received the promise of the Holy Spirit (cf. Jn. 20:20), the disciples returned to Jerusalem with great joy.

The cloud is a biblical symbol of the presence of God, of His glory, and of His protecting power. The risen Lord entered His heavenly glory in a heavenly carriage and sat at the right hand of God the Father. This was the last visible physical appearance of Christ to His disciples after the Resurrection. It is the end of His work in the divine plan of our salvation. Through the Ascension, Christ returned to the Father as He had often said that He would (Jn. 3:14-16; 12:32; 16:28; 20:17). His next glorious appearance will be in His Parousia, in His Second Coming.

In the Ascension of Christ, we have a vision of divine realities and actions. It speaks about God, man, and our relationship with God. Visibly we see how Christ the God-Man was lifted to heaven, and how heaven, man, and God are united in the Person of Christ. Christ came from heaven and has ascended to heaven, but now He has raised up to heaven His human body as well. St. Paul says it well when he writes: "God made us alive together with Christ... and raised us up together, and made us sit together in the heavenly place in Christ Jesus" (Eph. 2:5-6). In Christ the human and the divine nature are united and in Him, the whole of humanity is reconciled and united with God. Christ opened the way to heaven and gave us the power to walk the way to God, for He is indeed the Way to God. For this He was sent into the world, to call us back to the Father and to become partakers of the divine nature, to share in the life of God (2 Pet. 1:4).

The risen Lord ascended into heaven, where perfection and holiness exist. There in heaven, Christ sits "at the right hand

C. OUR SALVATION THROUGH THE PASSION OF CHRIST

of the Father," in "the bosom of the God," enthroned as Savior, Lord, and God. He received every authority in heaven and on earth. Heaven and earth are one world of God the creator.

Soon after the Ascension, on the day of Pentecost, Christ sent the Holy Spirit upon the Apostles and He is now with us until the end of the age, directing and protecting the Church (Mt. 28:18-20; Acts 2:2-4; Rev. 19:16; Rom. 8:34; Phil. 2:11; Eph. 1:20-23; Ps. 109). The work of Christ continues through the Holy Spirit in the Church until we see Him again coming with glory in His Parousia, in His Second Coming for the fulfillment of all things (Mt. 24:30; 1 Cor. 11:26; 15:51-58; 1 Thess. 4:15-17).

The Holy Spirit is working in the Church, sanctifying us and transferring us from earth to heaven, where we really belong. Especially in our Divine Liturgy, we experience our detachment from earth and our elevation towards heaven, where we live in communion with the Saints, with Christ, with God. It is in the Church where we become one with the Person of Christ, our Savior.

The Person of Christ and the Resurrection and the Ascension.

For three years our Lord spoke to the people about His unique relationship with the Father, His special mission on earth, and His elevation to heaven (Jn. 3:14; 6:62; 8:28; 12:32; 20:17). It is, however, in the events of the Resurrection and the Ascension that the Apostles saw Christ unfolding the mystery of the divine plan for the salvation of the world. The Resurrection and the Ascension illumined the mystery of the Cross and of the divine economy. The Cross and the Resurrection and the victory over sin and death belong to the eternal plan of God for the world. The prophets had foretold that it was "necessary that the Christ should suffer these things and enter into his glory" through His Resurrection and our own resurrection in Him (Lk. 24:22-27; Jn. 13:31-32; Rom. 8:11; 1 Cor. 6:14; 2 Cor. 4:14). With the Resurrection "all things were filled with light, heaven and earth and the regions below the earth." In the light of the Resurrection we see that the Incarnation and the Passion are the plan and work of God for the salvation of the world, a plan and work that had been hidden in the eternal will of God. In God there are no time limitations, past, and future, everything is an eternal present, and the eternal plan was realized "when the time had fully come." When it was the proper time for the world to accept the Messiah-Savior, when the Judaic religion, the Greek paideia, and the Roman commonwealth had spread throughout the known world, then the Messiah-Savior came into the world to begin His work of salvation. Christ, in love and obedience, gave Himself to save mankind (Mt. 26:26-28). The Resurrection of Christ was the glorious crowning of His saving work and a proof that His sacrifice on the Cross for the life of the world was accepted by the Father, and that He had now indeed entered into His heavenly glory.

C. OUR SALVATION THROUGH THE PASSION OF CHRIST

Thus the Apostles experienced the events of the Resurrection and the Ascension, and they expressed their experience in words and symbols so that we also may believe that indeed "God was in Christ reconciling the world to himself" (2 Cor. 5:19-21; Lk. 24:49-53; Acts 1:9-11).

This is the unfathomable depth of the Cross as the Apostles experienced it after the Resurrection and as the Church lives it to this day. God does not ask for satisfaction of justice. He loves and wants to save his lost children. He is therefore working eternally to save His world, to lead the world to its destiny, to make it the kingdom of God in cooperation with the free human beings. When the free children are in danger of being lost, the heavenly Father condescends, becomes man, and even suffers in the flesh in order to rescue them and raise them to His side in heaven. This is what any earthly father or mother would do for their children.

Spiritual ascent, then, is the call and the message of the Resurrection and the Ascension of Christ. We are called to be lifted up to where Christ and the Saints are, up a little higher from the earth and closer to God, to have communion and union of earth and heaven, creature and creator. There in heaven is where we belong, not on earth with the animals. We are images of God and rulers of the earth, but citizens of heaven. In the Divine Liturgy, we are again and again invited: "Let us lift up our hearts to heaven!" Let us indeed lift up our hearts to heaven! Without this sublime vision of heaven, our life remains in darkness, in spiritual poverty. But with this vision of heaven, our life on earth becomes a heaven, resplendent with divine light and joy in the Holy Spirit (Rom. 14:17). "It is the Spirit who gives life" (Jn. 6:63). May the Holy Spirit lift us up toward our Lord and Savior now, that we may be with Him and He with us always.

The Eternal Character of Christ's Sacrifice

The work of Christ is a work of God and has an eternal character and validity. The sacrifice on the Cross and the Resurrection of Christ took place in history once and for all time; they are unique events which cannot be repeated. But the saving power and energy of the Cross and the Resurrection continue the salutary work eternally on earth and in heaven, the one and indivisible world of God. In heaven the God-Man Christ remains always as the sacrificed Lamb for the salvation of the world and as the eternal mediator and high priest, always living and praying for the people for whom He died, and saving those who would approach God through Him (Heb. 7:24-28; Rom. 8:34; Rev. 5:6-14). On earth, Christ governs the Church through the Holy Spirit. He sent the Holy Spirit from the Father to remain with the Church and to guide it toward the fullness of truth, to make it "the pillar and bulwark of the truth" (1 Tim. 3:15; Jn. 16:13; Rom. 8:13).

The Church is the kingdom of God in the process of becoming. In the life of the Church Christ unites the whole world to Himself. The Church presents the Gospel of salvation. The

C. OUR SALVATION THROUGH THE PASSION OF CHRIST

people respond with faith to the love of God and enter into the mystery of the divine plan for the salvation of the whole world. With prayer and worship, they become one with Christ and through Him become one with God and the kingdom of God is fulfilled (Jn. 17:20-23). In Baptism we die with Christ and are raised up to a new spiritual life. With Confession, we are cleansed from the daily sins that we commit as weak human beings. These are the "dust" that we get on our feet (Jn. 13:8-10; 1 Jn. 1:8-10), and which must be shaken off, washed, and cleaned.

In Holy Communion, which Christ Himself has asked us to receive, He is Himself again present as the eternal high priest and as the sacrificial Lamb. He is at once "the offerer and the offered." With the invocation of the Holy Spirit, we have before us the presence of our Savior Jesus Christ. We receive His body and blood and share in His redeeming sacrifice unto remission of sins and eternal life; unto communion of the Holy Spirit and fulfillment of the kingdom of God. In Holy Communion we are nourished spiritually, we are forgiven and saved (Mt. 26:26-29; Lk. 22:15-19; Jn. 6:51-58; 1 Cor. 11:23-26). This is salvation: to be united with Christ and to become "a dwelling place of God in the Spirit" (Eph. 3:19-23; Jn. 17:21-23). In our worship, we really experience the kingdom of God on earth, as a communion of people where everything is done within the love of God and with the life of Christ, the leader, and perfecter of our faith, as our unique model and guide. Earth and heaven, men and angels, all together, we worship God and experience the kingdom of God on earth.

This life in Christ will be perfected at the glorious Second Coming, the Parousia of Christ, and in the new life in the kingdom of God. It is to this blessed end that all the prayers of the Holy Eucharist direct us, to "that day" of the kingdom of God. There and then we will find the perfect Communion; we will see Christ as He truly is, and we will become like Him (1 Jn. 3:2; 1 Cor. 13:12).

He Will Come Again

Christ came to us as Man and He is with us in the Holy Spirit to the close of the age. We live and breathe in the new sphere of His love and the kingdom of God is fulfilled in our life. But He will come again in His glory, as the Apostles have seen Him going up into heaven, with His divinized body and its wounds (Lk. 24:39; Jn. 20:25; Acts 1:7). Christ will come again to take us with Him forever (Jn. 14:1-3; 1 Cor. 15:22; 1 Thess. 4:16-18).

As God-Man Christ will be the King and Archpriest for the new humanity in the eternal kingdom of God. The kingdom of God and the kingdom of the Son is one. One is the throne and one is the glory of the Father and the Son (Col. 1:13; Rev. 21:22-24; 22:3-5). We will see the glory of God in the face of our Lord Jesus Christ. Our life will be an eternal liturgy.

C. OUR SALVATION THROUGH THE PASSION OF CHRIST

This is the divine economy for our salvation. In the divine plan for our salvation, we have seen how God is always working it out: The Father through the Son in the Holy Spirit saves His world and us.

6. The Divine Plan of Salvation in the History of the World

Man has always wondered about and philosophized on the universe. He sees the uninterrupted eternal movement of all things and asks: from where does all this movement originate, and where does it all lead? What is the ultimate cause? Movement, change, and decay are the main characteristics of the created world. Created things "are ever becoming and never really perfect beings," Plato said. He considered ideas as a real world. All things are in motion to reach their idea, their perfection. Aristotle postulated a first principle, the unmoved mover, which attracts everything and holds everything together.

Many people believe that behind this rhythmic movement of the world is God, the creator, and ruler of all. God is the unmoved, unchangeable being who guarantees and secures the world.

Christian faith, in the light of revelation and especially in the divine economy of our salvation, has its own thinking or philosophy on the same questions. We believe and know that God the Father creates and saves His world through His Son and the Holy Spirit. God has created the world, heaven, and earth in time, and He governs it providentially to its final goal. God said, "Let there be… and it was so" (Gen. 1:1-31. Jn. 1:1-3). This must be the "big bang" of the beginning of the world of the scientists! With the Word of God, the world came into being, and it is still in the process of becoming until it will be truly a "cosmos," an orderly and harmonious world, as it is destined to become. God created the world with a purpose and He will not fail. Faith sees the beauty of the creation and exclaims: "O Lord, how great are thy works, in wisdom hast thou made them all" (Ps. 104:24).

God created man in His image, a free spiritual being destined to have dominion over the world and to live in faith, obedience, and communion with God the creator. Man was destined to grow, in cooperation with the divine grace, to reach the likeness of God, in full knowledge of and closer communion with God (Gen. 1:25-30). The whole of humanity is moving to reach its perfection, to become the kingdom of God, to become a perfect community living in faith and love within the eternal love of God. This is essentially what all humanity is longing for.

Sin has interrupted this movement toward perfection. Man's disobedience to the will of God brought separation from God and consequently corruption and death. God in His caring love condescended, and in His Logos-Son, who created man in the first place, took the form of a slave and became man in the Person of Jesus Christ to free man from the slavery

C. OUR SALVATION THROUGH THE PASSION OF CHRIST

of sin and death. In the Old Testament, God was sending His Spirit to guide His people. Now the Logos of God, the personal wisdom and power of God, became man to save mankind. He took upon Himself the human nature; He sanctified it and elevated it in Himself to heaven, at the right hand of God. There He continues to reign over the world, directing it to its ultimate end, the kingdom of God (Mt. 28:18-20; 1 Cor. 15:23-28; Rev. 20:1-5).

The Economy of the Fullness of Time (Eph. 1:10)

The salvation through Jesus Christ was a mystery hidden in the will of God, "in the abyss of the silence" of God, unknown even to the angels, and now revealed as a historical reality in the Incarnation and the establishment of the Church. In Christ, the eternal love of God proceeded from His blessedness to visit His people personally (Lk. 1:68; 7:16). The divine Logos who once created man now becomes man to save all mankind.

While in prison for the Gospel of Christ, St. Paul meditates upon the work of Christ and its place in world history. He sees how God the creator economized the times as a good steward, accommodated the various periods of history, to reach the point of the fullness of time, and finally to send the Savior into the world. He sees how God selects great persons, Noah, Abraham, Moses, the Prophets, and how, through them, He leads humanity to its final goal, to become the one kingdom of God. St. Paul sees the Incarnation and the establishment of the

Church as the last epoch in world history. All historical events before were a preparation for the time of Christ, an education of humanity to accept Jesus Christ as Savior (Gal. 3:24-47; Jn. 1:29-51; 5:31-47). Christ and the Church is the last call of God for faith and union with God.

Through the life of Christ, and especially His Cross, the whole of humanity is forgiven and reconciled with God (2 Cor. 5:19-21). In the life of the Church, all people, mystically united with Christ, are on the move to become the one kingdom of God in heaven and earth struggling human beings of faith, angels, and saints together with our Lord Jesus Christ, as king and high priest forever.

This is the mystery of our faith: the recapitulation and union of all, heaven and earth, in the Person of Christ, one body, one flock, one shepherd Jesus Christ as leader over all, to the glory of God the Father (Jn. 10:16; 17:23; Phil. 2:11; Eph. 1:21-23).

The Self-Revelation of God in the Person of Christ

We know God only as He reveals Himself to us in His actions in creating and governing the world. A God who does not act and do things does not exist. The greatest action of God in the world is the extraordinary event of the Incarnation for the salvation of His people. In the Incarnation, the Cross, and the Resurrection of Christ we have a real self-revelation, a self-dis-

C. OUR SALVATION THROUGH THE PASSION OF CHRIST

closure of God as Holy Trinity. In Christ, we do not have just a teaching about God, but a theophany, an appearance of God. Christ bore witness to God the Father, not so much by His words, but by God Himself being present in the Son so that we could see God in Christ. God speaks for the Son not only by His words (Mk. 1:11; 9:7), but by His presence in the Son. God, present in the Son, gives Him the words and does the works which witness to Christ (Jn. 10:30; 14:8-11). The personal presence of God in Christ is a self-revelation of God as Father, Son, and Holy Spirit in the work of our salvation. Our salvation in Christ is the work of God the Holy Trinity, for "God was in Christ reconciling the world to himself." And He gave us the ministry of reconciliation (2 Cor. 5:18-21). The Holy Spirit now fulfills the work of salvation in the Church.

This is the essence and the heart of Christian faith: God became man in the one Person of the Holy Trinity in order to save His world. In Christ, we have "God with us."

God is one: the Father who has His Logos-Son and His Spirit, and through them creates and saves His world. The Son and the Spirit are and act as distinct Persons; they are sent into the world and they speak to the people as persons, but they are always one with the Father.

Do we understand rationally all of these things? They are matters of faith, and they belong to the heart, not to the mind. They have been revealed by the Holy Spirit to persons of faith and love. Once believed, they shed much light to our life and to the world. They reveal to us the full meaning of our life, where we come from, and where we are going (Jn. 8:12; 12:35-36). We also know that we are not just a piece of this world; we are not alone in this vast universe. We live here as unique persons in a unique relationship with God and we look forward to a brighter future life, sharing the glory of God and our Lord Jesus Christ (Jn. 17:24).

How About Our Dogmas?

The dogmas are not human knowledge. They are human expressions of what faith has experienced as reality. The dogmas and Sacred Scripture are the ark, the vessel that holds the treasures of our faith. They hold Christ, who is our treasure, the presence of God in His unfathomable love for mankind. Our treasure is Christ, the God who became man for us. The dogmas and the Scriptures are the means and the lens through which we have to look, find and live Christ, and thus have life in Him. All of the life of the Church, the Church itself, is the ark of the New Covenant, where we live in the presence of God and share the divine grace in Jesus Christ, and where we live our faith in Christ. We do not worship the ark, the dogmas, the Bible, and the Divine Liturgy, but without the ark, we lose the treasure; we lose Christ Himself. One cannot find Christ outside the life of His Church, His Body. Some people tried to find the "Jesus of history" outside the faith of the Church, but they did not find Him because He is not simply man; He is God who became man for us, and who is truly God-Man.

C. OUR SALVATION THROUGH THE PASSION OF CHRIST

You can live in the ark of the Church and go as deep into the truth as you can, or you can fly up as high as you can, but you cannot do anything outside of the Church. We only build upon the life of the Church (1 Cor. 3:5-15).

St. Gregory the Theologian (P.G.36,146C) sees how God, as a good pedagogue, educates His people throughout history. There are three states of transformation of the human way of life in the course of history. These three great events have changed the course of human life. The first great event in history was the Mosaic Law. The Law marked the transition from idols to the faith and worship of the true God. The second event was the transition from the Law to the Gospel, with the faith that salvation comes not by the works of the Law, but by the grace of God in Christ. The third earth shaking event was Pentecost, the period of the Holy Spirit in the Church, where we have the change from the present state of things to what lies unmoved and unshaken beyond, in the transcendent and eternal kingdom of God (Heb. 12:27-28; 13:14; Rev. 21:10-11).

This then is the plan of God in history: creation, Mosaic Law, Christ, the Holy Spirit in the Church, transformation in the Holy Spirit, and, through the general Resurrection, the fulfillment of the kingdom of God.

Is Christ God?

This question presupposes another serious question: Do we know what God is so that we can speak about the divinity of Christ? One loses his mind when he tries to think what God is, or what God is like. God is spirit, invisible and incomprehensible, according to the faith of the Church. God is the wholly Other and man cannot know Him in His essence (Jn. 1:18; 1 Tim. 6:16). We know God only in His energies, as He comes to us in His actions of creation and salvation of the world. We know God in His relationship to us. We see God in the beauty of the world in which we see order and harmony and we call it cosmos. We also see God in the majesty of man, created in the image and likeness of God, with mind, freedom, and the authority to rule over the world, as well as the possibility to know and to be united with God (Gen. 1:26-28; Heb. 2:6-8).

Above everything else we know God in His action for our salvation in Jesus Christ. In His love, God comes out of His eternal blessedness and creates the world through His Word-Logos-Wisdom. Now, in the same Logos, God comes out of His blessedness, receives human nature, and becomes man, to save man from sin and death. In the Person of Christ, we have seen God in all of His paternal love. With the eyes of faith, in the Person and work of Christ, we have seen the only Son of God in the fullness of the glory of God; we have seen the real "image of the invisible God... For in him dwells the whole fullness of God" (Jn. 1:14; Col. 1:15; 2:9). In the work of Christ we have seen that God saves us through His Son Jesus Christ (Jn. 3:16; Col. 1:12-14; 1 Cor. 1:30). Christ saves us, and therefore faith answers the question about Christ's divinity with its resounding yes!

C. OUR SALVATION THROUGH THE PASSION OF CHRIST

If He can save me and sanctify me, He must be God. But He is not simply God, nor simply a man. He is God who in time became man to save man. He is Theanthropos-God-Man. He is the Logos of God who is from the beginning, who is God, and who in time became man for our salvation. The Apostles and the Fathers never stopped emphasizing both the divinity and the humanity of Christ. Christ is Son of God and Son of Man, the Son of David in the flesh (Rom. 1:4; 9:5; Phil. 2:6-11). "In the beginning was the Word and the Word was God... and the Word became flesh" (Jn 1:1-14). Christ, the Logos, existed and exists eternally "in the bosom of the Father," "in the form of God," and in time He received the form of a servant; He became man, born of a woman. He became man but He is not one of us; He is not of this world. We cannot describe Christ as a man or even as a unique personality in the world. Christ is something more. He is far superior to Moses and all the prophets. The prophets are the servants of God. Christ is the unique Son, the inheritor of the vineyard of God; He is the vine (Mt. 21:33-38; Jn. 15:1-8; Heb. 1:1-8; 3:3-6). His relationship with the Father is unique. Christ refers to God as "My Father" not as "Our Father" (Lk. 2:49; Jn. 5:19; 20:17). If we could know what God is, we could also say what exactly the relationship of the Son with the Father is. He spoke about the kingdom of God and helped us to see that through Him and in Him the kingdom of God has begun. In Christ, God truly entered the world, even though He was never outside of the world. God entered history personally in the Son. The Son was sent by the Father to fulfill the work which the Father gave to Him to do, namely our salvation. And He returned to the Father to receive the glory which He had before He "emptied" Himself for us (Jn. 1:1-14; 16:28; 17:4; Gal. 4:4; Phil. 2:6-11). He did not just come simply to teach us, but to save us. He is our Savior and our Lord. His mission is the salvation of the world. He forgives sins and gives life; He saves and judges the world, and this implies divinity Thomas confessed; "My Lord and my God." And the Church believes and worships Christ as the Incarnate Logos, the Theanthropos.

God-Man is the special characteristic of Christ. He is one Person, Jesus Christ, in two natures unconfused, indivisible, and inseparable forever. If someone denies one of His natures, he denies our very salvation as the work of the loving God in Christ. It is this God-Man Christ that God the Father has made Lord and king over the world He has saved (Mt. 28:18; Acts 2:36; Phil. 2,8-11). The world was created for man. Man was created for God, and Christ brought man back to God (1 Cor. 15:25-28).

This is the Son of God of Christian faith. This is our salvation, a work of God the Father, through the Son, in the Holy Spirit. We see God only in His actions, and especially in His action for our salvation. If we cannot feel the presence of God working in the history of His world, we will also not be able to see that "God was in Christ reconciling the world

C. OUR SALVATION THROUGH THE PASSION OF CHRIST

to himself" (2 Cor. 5:19-21; Col. 1:20). Consequently, we will also be unable to think appropriately of God and of man, whom God loved so much (Jn. 3:16; Rom. 5:8). In the Person and work of Christ, we have seen the paternal love of God and the majesty of man as the beloved image of God. In His Person and in His life we have also seen the glory of God in all its fullness. And we will see it in the kingdom of God in eternity (Jn. 1:14; Mt. 17:1-8; Rev. 5:21-22).

One may wonder how men of God have seen the words and deeds of Christ and how they have understood them in the framework of the God-Man relationship in Christ. How have they seen man as God sees man and his destiny in life? How have they understood the works of God in Scripture? "Thus it was written... that Christ would suffer these things and enter into his glory" (Lk. 24:26). Men have been tempted and have fallen, and the Son of God who exists in the form of God took the form of man, took the place of man, was tempted Himself, so as to be able to help man to overcome temptations; He died so that we can have life in Him. How have men of God understood that the righteous and holy God can justify and save the unrighteous man? How have they understood that out of the humility and suffering of Christ can come glory for Himself, for us, for God, and true life in abundance? The answer is: They were holy men of God who spoke, being moved by the Holy Spirit, and we follow them (2 Pet. 1:21).

The Person and work of Christ is a great mystery (1 Tim. 3:16) that covers God, man, and our interrelationship with God in Christ. The mystery is not contrary to reason, but beyond our reason, and is understood only by inspiration. As our Lord said, "No one knows the Son except the Father, and no one knows the Father except the Son and anyone to whom the Son chooses to reveal him" (Mt. 11:25-30). No one has ever known what God is in Himself. The Church from the very beginning lives our salvation in Christ and worships God, Father, Son, and Holy Spirit, without asking for the "percent" of divinity in each of the three Persons of the Godhead. We cannot enter the inner life of God. Without the Christ of the Church we cannot speak seriously about Sacred Scripture, nor about God, because both belong to the believing Church. Without the Christ of the Church, we know neither God nor man for whom God cares so much. Without Christ, the Theanthropos, all things become an obscure myth, a darkness. Whereas in Christ, as the Church sings, "all things have been filled with light, heaven, and earth, and the regions below the earth" (Third Ode of the Resurrection Canon; in. 1,4-9; 8,12).

The basic question in matters of faith is: Do we believe in a living God, acting and caring for His world? If we can say Yes, then we can also speak about Christ as God-Man. When one lives the faith of the Church and feels the redeeming love of God in Christ, he does not need to ask for logical explanations of the great mysteries of God, Christ, and man. Faith is

C. OUR SALVATION THROUGH THE PASSION OF CHRIST

life, and life does not need too many explanations. Man feels the presence of God and worships God with awe, as he attempts to obey and imitate Christ as much as he can. This is Christian faith and life.

The Life of Christ and the Life of Man

Man was created in the image of God to live in communion with God and to present God as person. Only in man, in his pure heart can one see the image of God. Christ is the natural, the perfect image of God. In Christ, the Theanthropos we have seen God the Father (Jn. 14:9), as well as man in all his majesty and in his perfect relationship with God. Christ was the archetype for the creation of man, as He is the ideal and the goal of man: "To be conformed to the image of his son" (Rom. 8:29), to become Christ-like in faith, in love, and in obedience to the love of God (1 Cor. 15:28; 1 Thess. 4:17). Our hope to be with God in Christ for all eternity determines the way of our earthly life (Eph. 4:1; 2 Cor. 4:16-5, 10; Heb. 11:16; 13:14; 1 Jn. 3:1-3).

Christ existed in heaven. He came from above, from the Father, and became man (Jn. 1:14; Gal. 4:4; Phil. 2:6). He fulfilled His mission for our salvation on the Cross. He has risen from the dead and has gone back to the Father. He sits at the right hand of the Father and governs His holy Church in the Holy Spirit. We also come from above. There, in God, in eternity, is the root of everyone and of everything. Christ is our archetype and He is our final goal. We are born as human beings on earth, and we fulfill our mission in the history of the world. After our death, we go back to the Father, to eternity where we have come from, back to the bosom of the Father in the ocean of His fatherly love, with our Lord forever and ever. This is our root and our hope: up in God, not down in the dust. "The dead in Christ will rise first; then we who are alive, who are left (in this life), shall be caught up together with them in the clouds to meet the Lord in the air; and so we shall always be with the Lord. Therefore, comfort one another with these words" (1 Thess. 4:14-17; 1 Cor. 15:22, 51-58; Rev. 22:5). In this way, the Apostles have experienced Christ and in this way, the Church lives Christ and has life eternal in Him. The doctrines of the Church seek to present these experiences in as logical a way as possible and as truths and mysteries that are not contrary to, but above the revelations of the human mind.

It is indeed only in Christ that we can see man and his life in all its meaning and value. Let us, therefore, seek to know Christ the God-Man very well so that we can really know what we are. Let us believe in Him and follow Him in our lives here that we may also find ourselves in eternity with Him. "We are fellow workmen for God," and we are building on the cause of Christ until the whole world will become the kingdom of God. Amen! (1 Cor. 3:9-15; Mt. 11:28-30).

C. OUR SALVATION THROUGH THE PASSION OF CHRIST

Myths?

In periods of philosophical or scientific and technological advances, people very often lose their interest in matters of faith. They think that they have made progress, that they have come of age intellectually. They don't like to believe in things that cannot be proven scientifically. During the last century, some said that the stories about Christ are myths. For those who are outside the Church, the facts of Christ appear to be mythical because they are too great to be understood by their doubting minds; they are too good to be true.

There was a time when science sought to find the actual meaning that was concealed under the guise of a myth. Now that Christian Faith offers us the meaning of the world at its best, we are attempting to see it as a myth, as if afraid to look intently upon the light of Christ and to feel the love of God in Christ (Jn. 3:16; Rom. 8:31-39).

Everything around us and within us is a miracle myth beyond our understanding. We live this miracle every day and we think we know it. We study a few aspects of creation, and we think that we know enough and can control everything in the vast universe. This is nothing but the fool's pride of rationalism.

Myth was the poetic language by which people used to describe experiences of realities and relationships, which their heart felt as realities but which their mind could not express in ordinary language with its limitations (1 Cor. 2:6-10; 2 Cor. 12:1-10; Heb.11:1-3).

All Bible stories, from Genesis to the Book of Revelation, speak of the reality of the personal God-man relationships as historical events, as a panorama of history from creation, the Incarnation, and the life of the Church to the hope of consummation of all creation in the Parousia of Christ. The center of this history is the Person of Christ, His Cross, and Resurrection. The Christian story, lived and written in the light of history, brings out the truth of Christ in a clear and living manner. The Gospel of Christ will always be shedding light upon all the other stories and the myths of the world that are without God, especially if we read the Gospel to strengthen our faith and not to support our doubts.

According to the faith of the saved Church, however, Christ is the wisdom of God and the power of God unto salvation (1 Cor. 1:22-24). Christ is God who became Man for the salvation of mankind. And we live our faith in Christ in its most profound way in our Divine Liturgy, without any question as to the way we express the facts and stories.

Anthropomorphism?

Others, who don't want to take the teaching of the Apostles about Christ literally, can ask: Are all of these biblical expressions about God anthropomorphic? Yes, because only man, the anthropos, can understand and speak about God and man and their interrelationship. We are human and only in human terms can we approach the unapproachable divine.

C. OUR SALVATION THROUGH THE PASSION OF CHRIST

But in our human expressions, we must not lose the essence of our faith, i.e. the real man-God relationship. Religion and faith are indeed a man-God relationship. Are we thinking seriously about these realities? And if not, then what are we thinking about, since we are intellectual and spiritual beings capable of such sublime thoughts and experiences?

The Apostles were men and they lived the divine life within the Church; Christ Himself became man and used human language to speak of God the Father and to present the inexplicable God-man relationship, as a Father-Son relationship. Our purpose is to try to know and live this truth of our relationship, and not to be lost in words, in negative criticism. Research is good only if it helps us to see and live better the mystery of our relationship with God; it is not meant to shake the foundation of our faith.

The mystery of the Cross teaches us that God is the Creator and Father of all, and that He cares for His world. In Christ, He came to us in visible, physical form. He came to redeem us, to forgive, reconcile, sanctify, and bring us back home with Him so that we might not get lost alone in the struggle of life. And God gave man the power to work together with Him and to build the New Creation from within the old one (Jn. 17:16; 2 Cor. 5:17-18), and in this work, the Person of Christ is the ideal model of life. And Christ is still in the Church inviting us: "Be reconciled with God and with each other and have life!"

Can you believe and do this? Then bow and worship God in Christ. Try to live your life in Christ and you will see yourself in Christ. Only God knows man and only man can know God. We only need faith, eyes to see, ears to hear, and hearts to receive the truth. When we believe and live in Christ, then we can see the image of God in our pure heart (cf. Mt. 11:27), for we are indeed created in the image of God. And in the world, this is the highest honor of human beings: to be images of God, sons and daughters and friends of God.

D. OUR CHRISTIAN LIFE

1. *Divine Grace and the Gifts of the Holy Spirit*

Salvation in Christ is the work of divine love for man. This living love is called divine grace because salvation is based on the salutary sacrifice of Christ and not on our works. Grace is the undeserved love or favor of God for man. This truth is expressed clearly by St. Paul in his Epistle to the Ephesians "For by grace you have been saved through faith; and this is not your own doing, it is the gift of God - not because of works, lest any man should boast." (Eph. 2:4-10)

Divine grace is the saving and sanctifying energy of the Holy Trinity, the one Triune God, but it is particularly related to the Holy Spirit.

Everything in the life of the Church is accomplished with the help of divine grace. With faith and baptism the faithful receive divine grace and enter the realm of God's love where the work of salvation in Christ is continued in the Holy Spirit. When Christ completed the work of salvation with the Cross, the Resurrection, and the Ascension, He sent the Holy Spirit "who proceeds from the Father." The work of the Son prepared the way for the Holy Spirit to come, to continue, and to complete the work of salvation in the Church. The salvation accomplished by Christ is completed by the Holy Spirit in the world. The Holy Spirit is the cause of perfection and sanctification in the world. Sanctification is the purpose of the world and this is the main work of the Holy Spirit.

The Church sings: "The Holy Spirit provides all things." Everything in the Church is enacted by the Holy Spirit. The Holy Spirit selects the apostles and guides them in their missionary work. The Holy Spirit provides presbyters and bishops for the Church. The Holy Spirit opens the hearts of the faithful to know Christ and to confess Him as Savior, Lord, and God. In the Holy Spirit, we are united with Christ, and through Christ, with God, the Father to become "a temple of God in the Holy Spirit." (1Cor. 6:19)

The Gifts of the Holy Spirit

The entire life of the faithful is charismatic and this means that we live by the grace and the gifts of the Holy Spirit. St. Paul, however, distinguishes certain gifts of God, certain charismata, which make man capable of offering a particular service in the life of the Church. The Holy Spirit gives to each person a gift analogous to the work he is called to do in the

D. OUR CHRISTIAN LIFE

Church: to preach, to teach, to heal, to administer. Everything in the Church is done with the grace of the Holy Spirit. Every faithful person has some gift. All these gifts work harmoniously for the common good, the unity, and the progress of the Church, which is the Body of Christ. The proper exercise of each gift reveals the presence and activity of the Holy Spirit in the Church. Each person should be thankful to God for the gift he or she has received and should use it for the good of the community, never in a selfish way for his or her own good. All of the gifts are good and useful for the life of the Church. Thus no one should complain that he received a lesser gift, and no one should be prideful as having received a greater gift, forgetting that he received it from God freely as a gift (1 Cor. 4:7). No one should "think of himself more highly than he ought to think, but to think with sober judgment, each according to the measure of faith which God has assigned him" (Rom. 12:3). Pride tears apart and destroys the prideful person and the Church. No one knows if the gift was given to him because of his own worth, or if the gift makes him capable of doing the work assigned to him by the Church. "No one is worthy" on his own account for the sacred work of the Church. It is the Holy Spirit that heals the sick, fulfills what is lacking, and enables each one to be an apostle, a shepherd, and a teacher to the people (Acts 13:4.9; 20:28; Mt. 10:20).

The Gifts of Prophecy and Speaking in Tongues

All of the faithful have some gift of the Holy Spirit. St. Paul, however, is particularly preoccupied with the two gifts of prophecy and speaking in tongues. Prophecy is the catechism and instruction for the "edification" of the community in the faith and in the godly life. Speaking in tongues is a particular gift; a few in Corinth "spoke in tongues." They spoke, "in ecstatic tongues." In no other Epistle does St. Paul discuss the practice of speaking in tongues (cf. Rom. 12; Eph. 4). On the day of Pentecost, under the inspiration of the Holy Spirit, the Apostles "began to speak in other tongues, as the Spirit gave them utterance"(Acts 2:4). What the Apostles actually spoke on that day of Pentecost, how they felt, what they understood, and what they said, we can discern only from the preaching of St. Peter (Acts 2:14-40). Even though those who listened were from different regions of the earth, they understood the preaching in their own language or dialect. They believed and were baptized in the name of Christ (Acts 10:46; 19:6). Nowhere else are the Apostles presented as speaking in tongues. In Corinth however, speaking in tongues does not appear to be the same as on Pentecost; the faithful do not seem to understand it. From the context, it seems that even those who spoke in tongues did not understand and did not interpret what they were saying. (cf. "...my mind is unfruitful" 1 Cor. 14:14). Thus there was no spiritual edification of the Church, but rather disturbance and disorder. This is why St. Paul is preoccupied with this particu-

D. OUR CHRISTIAN LIFE

lar matter and seeks to put a stop to it in the assembly of the Church, unless there is someone to interpret what is being said in tongues (1 Cor. 14,5,13,28).

It appears that the Corinthians placed the speaking in tongues in the forefront, as an obvious and impressive gift. St. Paul, however, places it last in the line of spiritual gifts: On the other hand, he places it first when he wants to emphasize that gifts without love are nothing (1 Cor. 13:3). St. Paul prefers to emphasize prophecy, teaching, and the edification of the faithful. "He who speaks in a tongue edifies himself, but he who prophesies edifies the church" (1 Cor. 14:2-6). The purpose of the Church is edification and not the demonstration of gifts. This is why St. Paul says, "in church, I would rather speak five words with my mind, in order to instruct others, than ten thousand words in a tongue"(1 Cor. 14:19). Speaking in tongues does not edify the mind of rational man. The mind does not understand and man remains "fruitless," is not edified, nor does he receive spiritual benefit. Moreover, St. Paul implies that there is something childish in emphasizing the gift of speaking in tongues. He says at one point: "Brethren, do not be children in your thinking; be babes in evil, but in thinking be mature" (1 Cor. 14:20).

Even Scripture shows that speaking in tongues is not practical (1 Cor. 14:21-22; Is. 28:11). By speaking in tongues we appear to the simple and to the unbelievers who visit us as though we are "speaking into the air," as barbarians, or even as madmen (1 Cor. 14,9,11,23). But on the contrary, when we are all properly teaching, then the simple unbeliever or the inexperienced Christian, entering the assembly of the Church, will be instructed by all. Enlightened by the Holy Spirit, shown the depths of his soul, and moved to contrite repentance, the believer will confess "that God is really among you," that in the Christian Church indeed the true God is worshiped" (1 Cor. 14:24-25). This, after all, is the purpose of the Church assembly, to help each other to believe and to be reborn spiritually (cf. Acts 2:37-41).

St. Paul continues to exhort the brethren: Because you love the spiritual gifts, try to become rich in the gifts that truly edify. Love, seek to prophesy, to edify each other. As for speaking in tongues, do not exclude it altogether, but have someone to interpret what is said. If there is no one to interpret, let the one who has the gift of speaking in tongues keep silent in the Church assembly. He may speak to himself in his heart and with God. And we have so much to say to God that we cannot tell it to others or even to ourselves. These are the "ineffable words" which the heart sees and understands when it rises to heaven (1 Cor. 2:9; 2 Cor. 12:4).

The way par excellence to success is the love of Christ. Love is the "fullness of the law" (Rom. 13:8; Gal. :13-15). Love can solve all the problems of the Church in Corinth and the Church in the whole world. This is why St. Paul gave us the extraordinary hymn of love in 1 Cor. 13. He concludes the epistle

D. OUR CHRISTIAN LIFE

with the exhortation: "Let all that you do be done in love" (16:14). In the experience of love we are called to understand and to practice all the other gifts that God gives us, and this for the edification of the Church.

Orthodox Charismatic Life

Religion needs liveliness and enthusiasm to live and to repel the resistance of the world. In the Church, St. Paul does not speak in tongues, but in the power of God. He speaks of the secret and hidden wisdom of God, "what no eye has seen, or ear heard, nor the heart of man conceived" (1 Cor. 2:4- 13). He does not boast of his gifts, except only when the Corinthians force him to do so, and then he boasts rather of his weaknesses that make him strong in Christ.

Today some "charismatics" want everything to be impressive, and they are not satisfied when they do not see a great deal of liveliness in the Church. Of course, we have to give special attention to this situation. St. Paul says that "not all speak in tongues." Now those who can may do so, but let them speak to themselves. And the Holy Spirit will continue to speak to all in "ineffable sighs." Our Church in general does not speak in tongues, but lives charismatically and with love, and that is why it is alive to this day, in spite of all the difficulties it has met in its history. Love, faith, humility, and service is everything in the life of the Church.

The entire life of the Church is charismatic. Divine grace activates the whole life and growth of the Church.

Particularly in the holy Mysteries, we partake of divine grace, are nourished spiritually, sanctified, united with Christ, and saved.

Everything in the Church is done in the Holy Spirit. In the Spirit, we come to know the truth and to express it in doctrines. In the Spirit, we live the faith "in psalms and hymns and spiritual songs, singing and making melody to the Lord with all our heart" (Eph. 5:19). We avoid intemperate movements and expressions. Everything is done appropriately and in an orderly manner (1 Cor. 14:40). All the services of our worship are the fruit of the deep faith of the Apostles and the Fathers of the Church. They are the noble means that help us to live our faith in Christ, for faith is true life.

The hymns and the prayers, written in the Holy Spirit and expressing clearly the content and the meaning of the Christian faith, edify the faithful spiritually. The faithful, however, must know well the content of the faith and live it to the fullness of its deep meaning for our life. We go to Church not as independent spectators, but as members of the Church, as committed Christian believers, to worship God together with all the others, as the one united people of God. In the context of worship, we live our faith in Christ as the Church has lived it for two thousand years, and we thus share and participate in the events which are happening there. We go to Church and there we meet Christ, we hear Him, we see Him, we are united with Him, and we are lifted up to be in heaven with Him, with

D. OUR CHRISTIAN LIFE

the angels and the saints (Rev. 5:13). Those who live the events celebrated in the Church find themselves indeed in a higher spiritual atmosphere; they live in the divine grace of the Holy Spirit, in the presence of God in the Spirit, in communion with God, the saints, and the angels. They are indeed those who "mystically represent the cherubim and sing the thrice-holy hymn to the life-giving Holy Trinity." And the Holy Spirit which is in them and surrounds them sanctifies them, makes them sons and daughters of God, and partakers of divine life to the extent that this is possible for man. Perfection is to be received in the future, in a perfect life when we will enjoy completely the glory of God in the Holy Spirit. "Then the throne of the Lamb will be in the heavenly Jerusalem and his servants shall see his face, and they will reign forever and ever" (Rev. 22:3-5; 1 Thess. 4:17). "Thanks be to God who gives us the victory through our Lord Jesus Christ" (1 Cor. 15:57).

This is the charismatic life of Christian faith, as the Church has lived it for two thousand years. In the life of the Church, we live our faith at its best. We first have to learn, to know, and to live our faith. In doing so, we can enjoy heaven on earth and be a light to the world.

Our problem today, with the secular education of our times, is that we try to live our faith in God with our minds, and not with the mystical experience of our hearts. It is this mystical experience of the heart that helps us to penetrate the mysteries of the faith and to share in the events celebrated in our divine worship. Consequently; many of our people do not go often to the church services and they do not receive enough spiritual nourishment and strength for the struggles of everyday life.

2. The Fruit of the Holy Spirit (Gal. 5:22)

The heart of our faith is our salvation in Christ by faith. By faith, we are united with Christ in His death and resurrection and are being saved. To put it in another form: by faith, we are grafted into the olive tree of Christ, or we become branches of the vine which He is. Then we have to bring forth the proper fruit.

All fruit-bearing trees must bear fruit in abundance and of good quality. Every tree is identified by the fruit it bears. If the tree is sound it will bear good fruit. If the vine does not bear fruit, it is cut down and put into the fire and burnt (Mt. 7:17; 12:33; Lk. 6:43-45; Jn. 15:1-6). Every person and every society is the tree, the "fig tree" of God, which must bear certain fruit. The fruit for man consists of the virtues which he cultivates by the grace of the Holy Spirit. This is why I have chosen the passage of St. Paul where he calls all Christian virtues the fruit of the Holy Spirit. Everything in the Church is done in the Holy Spirit. Both the Prophets and the Apostles speak in the Spirit. We believe and confess Christ as Lord and God and Savior in the Spirit. In the Spirit, moreover, we pray and communicate with God, and in the Spirit, we become a

D. OUR CHRISTIAN LIFE

dwelling place of God. We live here in the Spirit, and in the kingdom of God, we will receive the Spirit in all His fullness. In this regard, St. Paul presents to us a group of Christian virtues: love, joy, peace, patience, kindness, goodness, faithfulness, gentleness, self-control, as fruit of the Holy Spirit. All of the virtues are an inspiration, an action, and the fruit of the one Spirit; all together they adorn the character of man. The Holy Spirit overshadows man, enlightens his mind and heart, and makes him capable of bearing much fruit, developing virtues, and becoming a personality. The Spirit of God illumines the spirit of man. The spirit of man is the mind itself, the heart, the inner man, as far as he is imbued and renewed by the energy of the Holy Spirit. Man is moved by the Spirit. This is why St. Paul admonishes: "Do not grieve the Holy Spirit of God (as person), but be filled with the Spirit," becoming strong and renewed in the Spirit (Eph. 4:30; 5:18; Rom. 12:2).

Love

The first fruit of the Holy Spirit is love. Love is the queen of all the virtues. Love is Christ, the king Himself. The life of the Christian is a dual love: love of God for man, and love of man for God and his neighbor (Mt. 22:37). God is love and comes to us as love. God's love for us arouses in us love for God and for our neighbor. Without this dual love, one cannot speak about Christian faith. Love gives essence and beauty to life. Without love everything in life is poor and ugly, unworthy egotisms, divisions, and wars (cf. 1 Cor. 1:10; 3:1; 13:1-8).

Love is a universal virtue, but it is in Christ that we reach the highest idea of love. In the Old Testament, we learned to love God and our neighbor. But the question always is: who is my neighbor? It is in Christ that we have learned that my neighbor is anyone who needs my help, or who can help me in my need (Lk. 10:29-37) and that we have to love everyone as we love ourselves. In Christ, we have learned that love is divine, that God is a loving Father, and that Christ is the love of God incarnate for us. The mystery of Christ is the mystery of the love of God and without love, we cannot grasp or understand it. In Christ, we are saved by the love of God and we are living in the love of God in Christ (Jn. 3:16; Rom. 8:31-39).

Love in Christ

We Christians learn to live and to love in Christ, for Christ wants us to live and to love as He has lived and loved us. "This is my commandment, that you love one another as I have loved you. Greater love has no man than this, that a man lay down his life for his friends" (Jn. 15:12-13). "Be merciful even as your father is merciful" (Lk. 6:36). "Be imitators of God as beloved children" (Eph.4,32-5,2). Love is not a matter of commandments; it is a way of existence, of life, an imitation of God Himself. We love people as beloved children of God for whom Christ died. In human beings we do not see race or classes and antagonism; we see the image of God, coinheritors of the glory of our Lord Jesus Christ who became man to find

D. OUR CHRISTIAN LIFE

the lost sheep and to bring it back to God the Father. In loving specific human beings we love God who so loves mankind (Jn. 3:16). It is in our love for people that we show our love for God who so loves us. There is just one love, the love of God and our love is a reflection of the love of God in Christ. We have a perichoresis of love, a mutual indwelling. The love of man exists and dwells in the love of God. In this divine origin of love in Christ, we have the ability to love even our enemies.

Love Is Absolutely Necessary for Our Life (1 Cor. 13)

St. Paul, who felt deeply the love of our Lord, presents love to the Church of Corinth as the only way for the survival and success of the Church. The Corinthians were blessed by many spiritual gifts of God: faith, knowledge of the truth, the working of miracles, and the gift of speaking in tongues. A one-sided emphasis on one gift over another created problems in the community, divisions, disorders, and scandals. St. Paul kindly, but clearly, criticized the knowledge of some Corinthians because it puffed them up instead of building up the faith and life of the community; rather he emphasized the need for unity and the purity of the Church. In chapter 12 of First Corinthians, St. Paul emphasized that the various gifts of the Holy Spirit are given to be used in a cooperative manner to create harmony and the building up of the Body, the Church, and not for personal pride. The situation in Corinth was difficult, and St. Paul thought that the only thing the Corinthians needed in this critical time was love. Love as the greatest gift of God is the only way and means to face problems and bring harmony in the life of the Church. Only Christian love can control the ego and pride of some people and make them humble and faithful servants, for the benefit of the Church of Christ. Therefore St. Paul wrote the 13th chapter of his Epistle, as a parenthesis between chapters 12 and 14. In 12:31 he writes: "But earnestly desire the higher gifts. And I will show you a still more excellent way." And love is the excellent way for ever higher achievements in our lives. Thus Paul saved for us the loftiest and most beautiful hymn of love.

The Necessity of Love

"If I speak in the tongues of men and of angels, but have not love, I am a noisy gong or a clanging cymbal. And if I have prophetic powers, and understand all mysteries and all knowledge, and if I have all faith, so as to remove mountains, but have not love, I am nothing. If I give away all I have, and if I deliver my body to be burned, but have not love, I gain nothing"(1 Cor. 13:1-13). First, Paul presents Christian love in contrast to other Christian virtues. he considers the speaking in tongues, so loved by the Corinthians and by some people even today. Then he takes the noble virtues of knowledge, faith, charity, and compares them with love in Christ. Paul speaks in the first person as if of himself and says: If I could possess all the gifts of the world, but missed the one, love, then I would profit nothing for my salvation. I would be nothing (for myself and for others), but a noisy gong or a clanging cymbal that merely bothers other people. There is indeed much knowledge

D. OUR CHRISTIAN LIFE

and eloquence, faith and charity without love, activities for showing off that perhaps can help others, but not ourselves. There can be faith that can perform miracles, but which does not have love (Mt. 7:21).

Without the ingredient of love, all the gifts we may possess, even in their most sublime form, are nothing, help nothing, make us nothing. Love is indeed the measure by which to assess the quality of our faith and life in Christ. Love is the very essence of Christian life (Jn. 13:34-35). All our virtues come out of love and lead to more love. Love is the one commandment that fulfills all the commandments and fills our Christian life (Rom. 13:8-10; Gal. 5:14; Col. 3:14).

The Qualities of Christian Love

After the dogmatic declaration of the superiority of love, Paul presents to us the various qualities of love; he paints out the beauty of love. He portrays to us the virtues of love. Love is personified: it is you and me, the loving Christian in our personal relationships with our brothers and sisters in our everyday life.

"Love is patient and kind; love is not jealous or boastful; it is not arrogant or rude. Love does not insist on its own way; it is not irritable or resentful; it does not rejoice at wrong, but rejoices in the right. Love bears all things, believes all things, hopes all things, endures all things. Love never ends." (1 Cor. 13:4-8)

Love Is Patient, as God is patient, waiting for our repentance. Love is kind, always gentle to all, and kindness is what our world needs in our days. Love is not jealous, envious, or boastful. The Christian does not envy the possessions and gifts of other people, rather he thanks God for their gifts to be used for the benefit of the community. Love lives for others. How much have families, churches, and nations suffered because of the jealousy and the boasting of some people! Love is not arrogant or rude; it does not behave unseemly and is always decent and gracious, kind and gentle.

Love Is Not Self-Centered, it does not seek its own rights, but the good of the many, that they may be saved (1 Cor. 10:24-33). Greatness is not in our possessions but in our unselfish giving. Peace and happiness are to be found in such unselfish giving of ourselves. Love always has a good temper. "When we lose our temper we lose everything. When we can master our temper we can master the world." Love never thinks of evil. If any wrong is done to love, love forgives and forgets. Love presents everything to Christ our Lord. Love does not rejoice in wrong things done to others, but rejoices in the truth, in the right thing. Love bears, believes, hopes, and endures everything. Love believes, trusts God and men. And our problem today is that we cannot trust or be trusted by people. Only God trusts us. Do we trust God?

D. OUR CHRISTIAN LIFE

Love Never Gives Up

Love always hopes for the best. Love never stops loving, even in persecution and suffering (cf. Christ, Paul, Stephen, the martyrs). Love never ends; it will continue to act even in the life hereafter into eternity.

Love is supreme over all other gifts. Many of the gifts of the Holy Spirit, as good as they are, are temporary and meant to serve the needs of the Church in its journey. Prophecy, knowledge, and speaking in tongues are all partial, imperfect. They point to the perfect to come. When the perfect comes, they will be less important, less needed. We see and know now only partly and dimly, as if in a mirror, as a reflection of reality. The time will come when we will see reality as it is; we will see Christ face to face (1 Jn. 3:2; 2 Cor. 5:7). Then we will see and understand things and persons fully. "Now I know in part; then I shall understand fully, even as I have been fully understood" (1 Cor. 13:12; cf. 8:3; Gal. 4:9; Acts 9:1-18). Only God who loves has known us fully.

Love is the Greatest

Finally, Paul comes to the three most important divine gifts, virtues: faith, hope, and love. They are abiding. They are special and they demand special attention. These virtues constitute the essence of our faith and they are necessary for the lives of all people, not only for some people. One can live without doing miracles, but one cannot be saved without faith, hope, and love.

Faith and Hope

We are justified and saved by faith, and we hope for the completion of our salvation (Rom. 8:24-25). Faith gives substance to things invisible and hoped for in the future (Heb. 11:1; 1 Cor. 15:19; Rom. 8:18-24). But love is the greatest, for love surpasses even faith and hope. Faith needs love to sustain it. And hope needs love to keep it warm and alive. Faith and hope without love become weak and faint. The time will come when we will see Christ face to face. Then there will be no more room for additional perfection of faith (2 Cor. 5:6-8; 1 Jn. 3:2). Faith will be changed into sight and hope will be replaced by realization; we will see the things we now hope for; we will enjoy the presence of God in a more splendid and perfect contemplation. But love will never end, for we will continue to love into eternity. "Love is a circle without end." Love has its end in itself. Love is the beginning and the end for every other virtue. All virtues come from love and exist to increase love, which will continuously remain and grow in perfection to reach the likeness of the love of God, who is love itself. Love will be life itself in the eternal kingdom of God. "So Faith, Hope, Love Abide, These Three; But the Greatest of These Is Love" (1 Cor. 13:13).

The Origin of Love

Love is the greatest gift and endures forever because its origin and essence is rooted in God who is called love and who is eternal. The inner life of the Holy Trinity is oneness in perfect love.

D. OUR CHRISTIAN LIFE

Love is creative and sacrificial. It goes out to give itself, to create life and beauty. Only God is able to love and create, and to recreate the world. The mystery of the world is love. Everything comes from love through love and for love (Rom. 11:36). The mystery of Christ is the love of God incarnate for our salvation. The name of God is love in action for the creation and recreation of the world. By the love of God we are saved, live, and have all the gifts of the Holy Spirit.

Thus only God loves and He is the source of our love. Our love is a reflection of our answer to His love for us. We love because we are His image and we have experienced His love for us (Jn. 3:16; 1 Jn. 4:10; Rom. 5:8; 8:15-39). Our love for God and Christ must be unlimited. Christ loved us to the end: He gave His life for us, His friends, and He wants us to love Him above the whole world, above our relatives, even above our own lives (Jn. 13:1; 15:12-13; Mt. 10:37). And we have to love our neighbor, for the love for our neighbor is the proof of our love for God. God does not need our love for Himself but for His people. The glory of God is the salvation of His people (1 Jn. 4:20; Jn. 17:1-3; Mt. 25:31-46).

Love in Christ

We can love people and the world only in Christ because in Christ we have experienced the love of God. In Christ, we see that "God so loved the world." (Jn. 3:16) We Christians live in the love of God and love in God. In Christ God has poured

His love into our hearts. Our love is infused with the love of God; we love in God. The more we feel God's love within our hearts the more we see and love people and the world as God's world. In the lilies of the field and the little birds of the air, we see the caring love of God the creator. In the people around us we see no races or classes or enemies, but the images of God, the beloved children of God, destined to become co-inheritors of the glory of our Lord Jesus Christ, who out of love became man and came to find the lost and bring them back to the Father, to become the likeness of God, gods by grace.

Love Our Enemies

In this love in Christ, the impossible for man becomes possible by God. A Christian must and can love even his enemies. For a Christian, there are no enemies, only brothers who "do not know what they are doing," and for them, Christ prayed and died on the Cross (Lk. 23:34; Col. 3:11-17).

In perfect love, man reaches the likeness of God who is love. This is the love of the Christian faith, and it is a gift of God brought to us by Christ. And this is what the Church offers to the world today: love, natural, spontaneous, limitless, indiscriminate, giving, and creative love, as God gives and creates His world. The beauty of love consists in giving and creating. And we can see in family life that real love is to give and create new life and love. We all need love in our life. People need love "for a smile" rather than bread. We are created to love and to be loved. Christian love is divine. It fulfills all the laws and it

D. OUR CHRISTIAN LIFE

fills our lives. And it is only through a fuller Christian love that we can overcome the worldly love of a selfish ego, grasping at power and possessions that spoils our lives and can never give real peace and happiness.

Life is love and we have learned it in the life of our Lord Jesus Christ. He is our teacher and our model of life (Mt. 11:29). Love is the greatest gift of God in our life; it is God within us. "God is love." He who would define this love is like someone trying with blurry eyes to count the sand in the ocean. To speak about divine love is to undertake to speak about God, and this may be dangerous for the unwary. But "love casts out fear" (1 Jn. 3; St. John of the Ladder).

Let us, therefore, desire earnestly the higher spiritual gifts, and let us practice love as the best way to reach this lofty goal. Let us learn from Christ about love. Let us make love the purpose of our lives, and let us love until we become love. For God is love and he who loves is born of God and knows God. If God so loved us we also must love one another. For if we love one another, God abides in us and his love (and joy) is perfected, completed in us (1 Jn. 4:7-12; Jn. 17:13-26).

Christian Joy

After love, St. Paul presents joy as a fruit of the Holy Spirit. Joy is the most desired thing in the life of man. Joy enriches and beautifies the life of man. Christians greeted and continue to greet each other today with the Greek: χαίρετε (kairete), rejoice!

Christianity is a religion of joy par excellence. At the Annunciation Mary was greeted by the angel with the Greek χαῖρε (kaire), "rejoice, hail, O favored one, the Lord is with you!" And at the birth of Christ, the angel greeted the shepherds with, "I bring you good news of great joy:" the joy of the birth of the Messiah-Savior who had been so awaited by the world. (Lk. 1:26-37) The Christian gospel was called εὐαγγέλιον (evangelion), a joyous message of God to man for the salvation of the world. Jesus began His ministry with the joy of the marriage in Cana, and His entire work was a gospel of joy. The kingdom of God, here and in eternity, is described with the image of a marriage banquet of joy and gladness (Mt. 9:15; 22:2; Lk. 14:16; Rev. 19:7; 21:9).

The joy of Christians is based upon the love of God for man, and on the certainty, we have an eternal life in Christ. There is great rejoicing in heaven for one sinner who repents and is saved (Lk. 10:17-24; 15:10-32). Christ experienced this joy as He walked toward the Cross for our salvation. "These things I have spoken to you, that my joy may be in you, and that your joy may be full... So you have sorrow now, but I will see you again and your hearts will rejoice, and no one will take your joy from you" (Jn. 15:11; 16:22; 17:13). The joy of Christ is our joy, and our joy is a joy for Christ, the ineffable joy of our personal relationship with God in Christ.

The Apostles experienced this joy of Christ on the day of the Resurrection of the Lord. The Apostles lived with this joy, and it is this joy which the faithful experience even during the

D. OUR CHRISTIAN LIFE

cruelest persecutions (Jn. 20:20; Col. 1:24; Phil. 2:1-4; 4:1-5). Christian joy is the inner serenity and happiness which the believer feels when he is aware in his heart of the love of God in the Holy Spirit. The believer enjoys this love of God in his life here on earth and with certainty looks to the future for the fulfillment of love and of joy in eternity. Nothing can separate us from this joy and this love. The unbelieving world can neither experience this special joy nor offer it; and certainly, it cannot take it away from the believer who possesses joy (Rom. 5:8-10; 8:35-39; Jn. 16:22).

This special joy, this happiness, and serenity we see in the faces of the Saints of the Church. We too have experienced this joy in worship from the time of the catacombs to the time of the magnificent Byzantine cathedrals. In our Divine Liturgy, Christ is there as the Lamb of God slain for our salvation, and all the faithful, living and dead, angels and saints, experience the love of God in Christ. Especially on Easter, the day of Resurrection, everything is filled with light, love, joy, and life. The love of God is made to be our love. We embrace one another in love, singing the hymn of joy: "Christ is risen." And this love fills us with joy and life. This joy is a foretaste of the eternal joy which we will experience with Christ. Thus, filled with joy, we will be able to say with St. Paul: Nothing in the world can separate us from the love of God in Christ Jesus our Lord (Rom. 8:35-39; 12:12-15; 14:17).

Joyful Sorrow

The kingdom of God is joy in the Holy Spirit and glorification of God for His love in Christ. What about the mourning or sorrow which the Fathers of the Church speak about? What is that? That is the sacred awe which man will always feel before God who is absolute holiness (Lk. 5:8; 18:13; Is. 6:5). Before the holy God, man is acutely aware of his spiritual poverty. He is "poor in spirit" and feels a certain sorrow in the presence of God that leads him to tears of repentance, to spiritual catharsis, and growth. The saint feels a certain sorrow for his imperfection, but together with the tears he also experiences an inner joy and delight for the forgiving love of God. This combined sense of contrition and joy is called χαρμολύπη (harmolypi), a joyful sorrow, by the Fathers of the Church. Those who live without Christ, "having no hope and without God in the world" (Eph. 2:12), are the ones who experience sorrow without the mystical joy of divine love. Sin is the only power that overshadows the joy of the believer, precisely because it separates us from the love of God. The Christian, however, knows that there is no sin that is greater than the love of God. God is our loving Father, and a father does not want his children to live in pain. There is need for a combination: sorrow in God for our shortcomings and joy in the Holy Spirit for the abundant love of God. If we have not tasted the joy, the serenity, and the happiness granted to us by our faith in the love of God in Christ, then something is missing from our faith and life. We still live

D. OUR CHRISTIAN LIFE

under the law, not under the grace and love of God (Rom. 6:14; 8:15). Our faith is weak. We do not live spiritually. We live far from the love of God and like the prodigal "perish here with hunger!" This is why it is necessary to return to the Father with repentance and confession and to begin a new life with joy in the Holy Spirit near God the Father of love. Life then becomes again a spiritual banquet (Lk. 15:17-33). This is the beauty of Christian faith and life, the love and joy in the Holy Spirit.

Let us, therefore, examine ourselves to see if indeed we live according to Christ, and if we do, then God will fill our souls with every joy and peace in the Holy Spirit. And on that day of judgment, Christ will say to us: "Well done, good and faithful servant... enter into the joy of your master" (Mt. 25:21).

Christian Peace

Another gift and fruit of the Holy Spirit is peace. Love, joy, and peace go together. None can exist without the other. Peace was and is the most desirable gift for man. And the greeting of our Lord, "Peace be with you," will remain the most beloved prayer for all of us. There are many types of peace: personal, familial, social, and international. And usually, peace means the absence of enmity and confrontations, and the presence of friendly relations among people and nations.

The peace about which Sacred Scripture speaks is the inner, the personal peace and serenity of the soul, which flows from the good and virtuous relationship the spiritual man has with his neighbor and with God who is the source of peace and serenity. This peace is founded upon the love of God and the certainty the believer has of salvation. The love of God banishes every fear and stress from the soul and grants a sense of security and happiness to man. We lost this peace in Paradise with the sin which separated us from the love of God. Only Christ lived this peace because only He as man lived His life in proper relationship with God the Father. The will of Christ was always the will of the Father. His "food" was to do the will of God and to complete the work of salvation for which He was sent into the world (Jn. 4:34; 17:4; 15:10; Lk. 22:42). It was this peace which Christ gave to His disciples on the evening of His betrayal. The night was a very difficult one both for Christ and for His disciples, and yet Christ said to them: "Peace I leave with you; my peace I give to you.... Let not your hearts be troubled, neither let them be afraid. Believe in God and believe in me" (Jn. 14:27). When we enjoy the right relationship with Christ, when we have Christ with us, then nothing can trouble our hearts. The presence of the love of God expels every fear and gives us inner serenity and calmness of the soul. This same peace Christ gave to the disciples immediately after the Resurrection, and the disciples gave it to the whole world wherever they preached the Gospel of Christ. In every Epistle, the Apostles wish this peace upon all of the faithful. "Peace be with all" is the main wish and prayer of the Church.

This is the peace of Christ. And it is a work of the love of God in Christ, a work of divine forgiveness and reconciliation with God and men (2 Cor. 5:19-21). It was this reconciliation, the res-

D. OUR CHRISTIAN LIFE

toration of good relations between God and mankind that Christ came to bring to earth, as the only mediator between God and men. Christ is our peace; He is the peace of God which surpasses every human thought. On the Cross, Christ destroyed all the partition walls of enmity and united all of us with God and with each other in a new man in Christ. It is this peace also which St. Paul speaks of in his letters (Eph. 2:14-18; Phil. 4:7; Rom. 5:2; 8:35-39).

To really live, man needs peace. Man has been created by God and for God, and his soul will not find peace unless it finds itself with faith and love near God. If we have not yet experienced the peace of Christ within us, this means that we have not taken our proper position within the love of Christ; we are not in a good relationship with Christ, who is our peace. We do not believe and we do not pray conscientiously. Therefore, we do not attempt to harmonize our will and our works with the holy will of God. We go our separate way, alone, in the pathway of life. This is why we experience distress and anguish. We need, therefore, a great deal more self-examination and adaptation to the will of God.

All the great men of earth promise and work for peace, and yet peace remains still an unfulfilled dream because we do not seek peace where we should and as we should. We do not found peace upon Christ, but upon human powers. Human powers are always weak, uncertain, and often destructive. Thus the peace we achieve is temporal, without love, and oftentimes unjust; it is more like revenge, punishment, and humiliation of the defeated, without the Christian love that can change the defeated for the better and call them to repentance and love. Such peace is a negative peace, a simple absence of hostilities, a temporary "cease-fire" after which we are ready for a still more cruel war. The peace of Christ, however, is a real peace, abiding and eternal, because it is founded upon the eternal love of God that embraces the whole world. Without the love and the peace of Christ in our hearts, peace and harmony will never come into the world. We will always have "sounds of war," distress and anguish, in spite of our scientific and technological successes. When the peace of Christ prevails generally over individual persons, then we can achieve the broader peace in the whole world.

Let us pray that God may enlighten us and the world leaders to know Christ better, and to establish peace upon the love of God in Christ. Blessed are the peacemakers. Let us seek peace, and the God of love, peace and hope will fill our hearts with joy, peace, and serenity (Mt. 5:9; Rom. 14:19; 15:13; 2 Cor. 13:11).

Patience, Kindness, Goodness

Love and peace bring with them the other virtues: patience, kindness, and goodness. All of the virtues are a fruit of the Holy Spirit and they all go together and complete the personality of the spiritual person. The virtues are all spiritual mosaics that adorn man as the image of God.

D. OUR CHRISTIAN LIFE

Patience, like kindness and goodness, is a virtue that shows the attitude of a Christian toward his fellow human beings. Patience is a gift in man that comes from the love and the respect we have toward our fellow human beings, revealing the nobility and superiority of our soul. The Christian, being noble and good, is not in a hurry to judge and to seek retribution for some mistake or injustice. He postpones judgment and waits in hope for the evil to be corrected. The patient person is "quick to hear, slow to speak, slow to anger" (Jas. 1:19).

Patience in its perfected form is the likeness of God. God who is love is also very patient, kind, and good and He loves mankind. God is kind to all of us, even "to the ungrateful and the selfish" (Lk. 6:35). God does not punish us for our mistakes, but is long-suffering and patient, waiting for our repentance and our salvation (Lk. 15:20-24; Rom. 2:4; 2 Pet. 3:9-15). God's patience, kindness, and goodness were revealed primarily in the Person of Christ. Christ did not come to judge and to punish, but to seek and to save "the lost," to bring us back to the love of the Father (Lk. 19:10; 1 Tim. 1:16; Tit. 3:4-7). If God Himself is patient and shows loving kindness, He requires that we too be patient, kind, and good towards others. We are created in the image of God and it follows that we too must reflect this goodness of God. "Be merciful, even as your Father is merciful" (Lk. 6:36). This is strongly emphasized in the parable of the unforgiving servant (Mt. 18:21-35).

The Apostles were patient, kind, and good in their apostolic work. They worked with patience, kindness, and genuine love because they had experienced in themselves the love and the patience of God Himself (cf. 2 Cor. 6:3-10; 1 Tim. 1:15-16). This is why St. Paul also exhorts us to lead a life worthy of the calling to which we have been called, "with all lowliness and meekness, with patience, forbearing one another in love... Be kind to one another, tender-hearted, forgiving one another, as God in Christ forgave you... Be imitators of God, as beloved children" (Eph. 4,1-2. 32; 5,1).

We live as a society, as a Church of Christ, and in our daily relationships we are confronted with differences of opinions and a whole variety of difficulties, and patience is the only way to remain united in faith and love. Many problems which seem to us very difficult today can be seen tomorrow to be so minute that with a little love they can be corrected altogether. And it is quite possible that patience and love can help both us and those who may have wronged to become better. It is indeed a terrible thing to see divisions and enmity within the Church of Christ, particularly if it is for insignificant and secondary things.

Patience, kindness, and goodness are indeed great virtues. They show the nobility and superiority of the soul, and they help greatly in preventing or correcting many problems. We will never regret showing patience in any given situation, but we will often feel sorrow and disappointment for having made quick judgments.

D. OUR CHRISTIAN LIFE

Let us, therefore, be patient, kind, and good toward our fellow human beings, as God Himself is patient and kind and good to us. Let us not permit ourselves ever to be overcome by evil, but rather let us overcome evil with good. The stronger ought to sustain the weaker members of the community, as Christ Himself carried and carries even now our burdens and weaknesses. "Let all men know your forbearance" (Phil. 4:5; Rom. 14:1; 15:1; 2 Pet. 1:5-11).

Let us all work together for the common good and not each person for himself. Let us forgive, for we must all be saved. Let us forgive and love each other so that we can experience more directly and truly the forgiveness and the love of God in Christ. In this manner, we will live a happier life, and the Church will maintain its unity, as the one body of Christ, with faith in the one God who forgives and unites all in His love.

Faithfulness, Gentleness, Self-Control

Three more virtues which adorn the personality of the Christian are faithfulness, gentleness, and self-control.

Faithfulness here means trustworthiness in one's relationships with fellow human beings. Trustworthiness is the reliance and confidence which other people have in us as Christians. Every person, and certainly the Christian person, must keep his or her word and faithfully fulfill any promises and obligations made to other people and to God. The Christian lives and does everything consistently before God and according to the will of God. His yes will always be yes, and his no will always be no.

Absolutely faithful and trustworthy in His promises to man is God Himself. All of our hopes of salvation are based on the absolute faithfulness of God and on His steadfast and abiding love for us. God remains faithful even when people are unfaithful (Rom. 3:2-4; 1 Cor. 1:9; 2 Tim. 2:12-13).

Faithfulness is essential in our daily life. Without it, we cannot live as a society. But even more so we cannot live without faithfulness as the Church of Christ. All of us must be faithful to our word and to the responsibilities which we undertake in whatever area of life. We must indeed live a life in Christ. Thus we will become an example in society and the Church will be the light of the world leading to Christ and to salvation.

Gentleness (Meekness)

In the world of egotism, ostentatious displays, and noise, in which we live, St. Paul, the Apostle to the Nations, projects the virtue of gentleness that should adorn every Christian soul, since it too is the fruit of the Holy Spirit. Gentleness and humility were the life of Christ as a whole, and as "an innocent lamb, without a cry" He was led to the Cross. This is why Christ invites us all to learn the lesson from Him: "Come to me all… and learn from me; for I am gentle and lowly in heart"(Mt. 11:28-30; 21:5; Acts 8:32). A person can be gentle and humble when he becomes a disciple of the gentle Christ. Then he will find rest and peace in his soul.

D. OUR CHRISTIAN LIFE

The gentle (meek) man is quiet, mild, calm, peaceful, noble, and pleasant in his conversations with others. His presence will always emanate serenity and peace. This is why St. Paul beseeches us in the name of Christ to behave "with all lowliness and meekness, with patience, forbearing one another in love"(Eph. 4:2). And when we speak to unbelievers we must defend our faith with firm gentleness and the fear of God (Gal. 6:1-5; 2 Tim. 2:24-25). It is only in this way, and certainly not with hysterical shouting, that we can hope to win the unbelievers to Christ. Gentleness and kindness are the main things our troubled world needs today.

Gentleness is indeed a jewel in the spiritual life of the believer. Let us learn to practice this great virtue from the Lord Himself and we will certainly see the beauty, the peace, and the serenity which Christian gentleness offers to our own life. "Blessed are the meek, for they shall inherit the earth" (Mt. 5:5), that is, the promised land, the eternal blessings of the kingdom of God.

Self-Control (Temperance)

As a final fruit of the Spirit St. Paul presents us with the virtue of self-control. Self-control is the ability of the free man to be self-determined, to have control over himself, to restrain and direct his natural drives and desires in a temperate way, and not to be led astray by his passions.

Spirit and Flesh

Man is a unified psychosomatic reality. Soul and body, spirit and flesh are the two elements which constitute the whole person, created in the image of God. There are two laws that work in man, the law of the spirit and the law of the flesh. We refer to man as flesh or body in reference to his natural impulses and passions. We refer to the same man as spirit in reference to his higher spiritual aspirations and desires. We call spirit the mind, the heart, the soul, the inner man, the higher and more spiritual self of man. Man is spirit to the extent that he lives under the influence and the enlightenment of the Holy Spirit.

Flesh and spirit are both given to man by God and they are very good. The flesh is not evil; it is created by God, and it is the dwelling place of the soul and the temple of the Holy Spirit. And the Lord Himself in the Incarnation received human flesh and deified it with His divine nature. For man to live in harmony there must be a harmonious cooperation between the flesh and the spirit. The spirit must govern and direct the flesh. Whenever the flesh acts independently of the spirit, when the passions override and do not follow the authoritative direction of the spirit, then we have disharmony in life and enmity between spirit and flesh. Moreover, we have a dichotomy of personality. Our soul seeks one thing and we do something else. This dichotomy in man is vividly described by St. Paul in his Letter to the Romans, chapter 7. This struggle between

D. OUR CHRISTIAN LIFE

the spirit and the flesh is something we all experience to one degree or another (Gal. 5:16-17). Therefore, we must neither deprecate or neglect the flesh, nor cater to it with unrestrained pleasures. The natural impulses of the flesh are of God and for a certain purpose. If we allow these impulses and drives to have free and uncontrolled expression, they become wild and lead to destruction. Excessive and unbridled indulgence of the natural impulses weakens the will for self-control in man. Man loses his personal freedom and becomes a slave of the world, of the material things that will never satisfy him. But when on the contrary the natural instincts are governed and controlled by the spirit, the mind, then man is called and truly is a person, the image of God. He lives a higher, more spiritual life, a life according to the will of God.

This, then, is the meaning of self-control: the ability of rational man to determine freely the values of life according to the will of God and to censure his natural passions and desires so that he maintains his personal freedom and control over himself. This is why St. Paul exhorts us to "walk by the Spirit, and do not gratify the desires of the flesh... If by the Spirit you put to death the deeds of the body you live... For all who are led by the Spirit of God are sons of God" (Gal. 5:16-24; Rom. 8:12-15). The faithful die to their lower selves and allow the Holy Spirit to build up the new man, the self that is being renewed "after the likeness of God in true righteousness and holiness" (Eph. 4:22-24; Col. 3:9-11).

Self-control must be practiced, therefore, in the areas of food and speech, anger and wrath, thoughts and acts of evil. We are all athletes of Christ, running in the stadium of virtues for the unfading crown of glory. "Every athlete exercises self-control in all things" (1 Cor. 9:24-27; Phil. 3:12-14; 2 Tim. 4:7-8).

Like a loving mother, the Church has set aside certain periods of time for greater spiritual self-control and asks of us a greater degree of self-examination and abstinence from certain foods and worldly pleasures. At the same time, the Church offers more opportunities for spiritual uplifting: gatherings for worship, prayers, confession, and more frequent Holy Communion.

Fasting must not be practiced mechanically by routinely abstaining from certain foods. Fasting needs to be practiced conscientiously with full awareness of our imperfections and out of love for Christ. With true, real fasting, we can grow spiritually and also be helpful to our needy neighbor. It was with such fasting that great men of the faith, such as Moses, Elijah, and the Fathers, were victorious in life.

Some may be inclined to ask us: Are we all to become ascetics? No. But neither must we become slaves to material things, to human weaknesses, and the worldly pleasures which can never satisfy us. The spiritually noble person knows the high purpose of his life; he respects himself and never allows himself to become a slave to his passions. He says with St. Paul:

D. OUR CHRISTIAN LIFE

"All things are lawful for me, but not all things are helpful. All things are lawful for me, but I will not be enslaved by anything" (1 Cor. 6:12-13).

The more one is liberated from the attraction of worldly things, the more he can progress spiritually. And the more one is subjected to Christ and to His will, the more one feels free and lives the presence of Christ in his heart (Gal. 2:20). The fullness of freedom and of perfection will be experienced in the Parousia of the Lord as a perfect and complete obedience to God. There and then we will have the perfect "freedom of the sons of God," a life in the infinite love of God from which nothing can separate us. And it is this perfect freedom that all creation waits to see.

Humility and the Saints of the Desert

Another Christian virtue is humility. Because the Fathers of the desert have a very high regard for the virtue of humility, we will present here some of their thoughts on this important subject. These Fathers call humility by the name of παναρετι (panareti), virtue of all virtues, holy humility, and mother of virtues. Humility together with love constitutes the sacred couplet of virtues. Love and humility are really one. Love is the queen of the virtues. Without love, man cannot be humble, and without humility, man cannot love. The devil cannot be humble because he does not love. Humility attracts divine grace. Therefore "dwell not with a prideful person that you may not lose divine grace from your soul." Humility is essential for our salvation; we cannot do without it.

Humility is an inner power that actually exalts, transforms, and sanctifies man. Pride made a few angels into devils. Humility makes angels out of devils. Humility is a spiritual whirlwind that can lift the fallen and raise him to heaven, guide him to the gate of the kingdom of God, which is Christ Himself, the ultimate humility. One can be saved without performing miracles or without having visions, but no one can enter the wedding feast without humility. Humility is an ineffable virtue and a gift of divine grace to the faithful, and we learn it from Christ (Mt. 11:29; 18:1-5). Humility is an imitation of the humility and the love of Christ. Someone once saw the beauty of humility in his heart and he asked her: "What is the name of your father?" And she answered: "He is anonymous and I cannot tell you until you have acquired God."

Christian humility, moreover, is not humiliating. It does not diminish the personality of man. First of all Christian humility comes from the feeling of the imperfection which the believer feels before the majesty of the absolute holiness and goodness of God. The humble person is "poor in spirit," recognizing his shortcomings and seeking to receive from God forgiveness, cleansing, and power to continue the spiritual struggle.

D. OUR CHRISTIAN LIFE

The humility that we see in the Person of Christ is not the humility that a lesser man might show toward his superior. This sort of humility is rather a natural virtue. Christian humility is for the stronger to condescend out of love and appreciation to help the weaker. "We who are strong ought to bear with the failings of the weak, and not to please ourselves" (Rom. 15:1). In the Person of Christ, we see how God bowed down from heaven to help weak man. Everyone who humbles himself for the good becomes "strong;" he becomes "in the likeness of God." And the Church always emphasizes both love and humility.

Humility and love are the virtues that can give us happiness in life, a life of paradise, of the kingdom of God on earth. In life, with humility and love for each other, we will realize the superiority of man and the majesty of the Christian faith, which believes in a God who, out of love, works for our salvation. Christ has taught us the power of humility and has shown it in His life. Let us learn from the Lord the way of holy humility, and let us imitate Him. "Let us put on humility, and humility, like a whirlwind, will lift us up to Christ, who is the ultimate humility." Amen. (Col. 3:12)

Love, joy, peace, patience, kindness, goodness, faithfulness, gentleness, self-control, humility, these are the abundant fruits of the Holy Spirit. These are the virtues that adorn each individual and make him or her indeed a person, an image of God: These are the virtues which humanity needs desperately today, tired and suffering as it is from the manifold pressures of life, with wars, evil, hatred, hypocrisy, and unbridled carnal pleasures that can never satisfy. The Church of Christ offers these virtues to all of us and requires of us our cooperation, because without our cooperation the love of God does nothing. The salvation of man becomes a reality in the cooperation between divine grace and the free will of the spiritual man.

Mankind has tried many systems of life and yet has not found true happiness and peace. Let us try the "system" of Christ. Let us take upon us the yoke of Christ as a rule of life, and we will surely see that His yoke is better than other yokes and that His burden is much lighter than all the other burdens with which leaders without Christ seek to burden us. In Christ, we will find true rest for our soul, for He is the only way, the truth, and the life.

The beautiful and bold exhortation of St. Paul sums up the essence of the Christian life: "Rejoice in the Lord always; again I will say, Rejoice... Whatever is true, whatever is honorable, whatever is just, whatever is pure, whatever is lovely, whatever is gracious, if there is any excellence, if there is anything worthy of praise, think about these things. What you have learned and received and heard and seen in me, do, and the God of peace will be with you" (Phil. 4:4-9).

D. OUR CHRISTIAN LIFE

3. The Armor of God
(Eph. 6:10-19)

So much in life is a struggle! There is a struggle for survival and a struggle for progress, even domination. So much is competition or even confrontation, economically, and politically. And there are so many national wars.

The kingdom of God, too, is a spiritual struggle. Religion is not the opium that puts people to sleep, but a spiritual struggle against the manifold enemy, "against the wiles of the devil" who instigates us to think and do evil things (Eph. 6:10-18). The kingdom of God is a gift of God in Christ. But Christ inaugurated the kingdom of God on earth as a movement and a revolution against sin and against moral and social evil. And this is a triple struggle: against our natural weaknesses, against the temptations of the secular society around us, and against demonic temptations. In the final analysis, the kingdom of God is a struggle for spiritual growth and perfection. Our forgiveness and reconciliation through the Cross of Christ are, so to speak, a new chance and a new opportunity to join our leader and fight for our goal. A Christian is called to grow spiritually, to become a saint, to reach the unreachable measure of perfection, and to become an imitator of Christ. This struggle has no end, for we can never reach the perfection of Christ (Eph. 4:13-16; Rom. 8:29).

The Christian Church presents itself as the army of Christ in the struggle against evil and for the victory of the kingdom of God. In this struggle, Christ the victor is the leader who conquered the power of sin and death with the Cross. After Christ comes the cloud of witnesses, the saints who followed Christ in the struggle. The saints in turn are followed by the faithful. All are soldiers and warriors for the kingdom of God, fellow fighters and athletes. Only the victors, those who fought according to the rules and won, receive the prize (Heb. 12:1; Jn. 16:33; Rev. 3:21; 1 Cor. 9:24-27; 2 Tim. 2:5; 4:7-8).

This spiritual struggle is particularly difficult because it is not a human struggle, but rather a struggle against the evil powers that cannot be overcome with mere human power. This is why St. Paul encourages us to put on "the whole armor of God" so that we may be able to stand against the wiles of the devil and be victorious in this spiritual war. "Therefore take the whole armor of God, that you may be able to withstand in the evil day, and having done all, to stand" (Eph. 6:13).

In every Christian, St. Paul sees a soldier of Christ. Using the Roman soldier as his example, he describes for us the spiritual weapons of the soldier of Christ: truth, righteousness, peace, faith, and prayer. Without these, we cannot stand in the battle. All of these weapons have to do with our life in Christ. St. Paul describes these Christian virtues by the poetic image of a soldier preparing for battle in order to reinforce their importance for our daily struggle in Christ and to challenge us to apply them effectively in our own lives.

D. OUR CHRISTIAN LIFE

Truth. "Stand, Therefore, Having Girded Your Loins With Truth."

(Eph. 6:14a)

The first thing a Christian soldier needs is a profound knowledge of the truth, which is Christ Himself (Jn. 1:14; 14:8; 17:3). The warrior needs to know why he is fighting. As the belt around the waist gives stability and power to the warrior, so also the true knowledge of the mystery of Christ gives us the power to stand upright and to win in the battle against temptations. He who does not know the truth of Christ well cannot live according to Christ and, "in time of temptation," is discouraged and tempted to desert and leave the battle; he falls, he is choked by the thorns of life, and does not bear much fruit (Lk. 8:12-15). Our Lord said: "And you will know the truth, and the truth will make you free" (Jn. 8:32). This is why it is necessary to read continuously the word of God and to listen carefully to the teaching of the truth of the faith, so that we can stand firmly and not be misled by the various spiritual and political currents of our time (Eph. 4:14).

Righteousness. "Put On the Breastplate of Righteousness."

(Eph. 6:14b)

Another defensive weapon in our struggle is righteousness. Righteousness has a double meaning. First, it means that God has made us righteous, has recognized us as being just;

He has saved us and is saving us freely because of our faith in Christ. Second, it means that we are to live according to the will of God, as it is expressed in Sacred Scripture and in the life of the saints. The Christian must hunger and thirst for the righteousness of God; he must live according to the will of God; he must live a life with faith, love, and reverence for God and for his neighbor. A Christian attains to spiritual perfection when he identifies his with the will of God when he can say with Christ: not my will but the will of God be done (Lk. 22:42). Such a life of righteousness is truly a breastplate that protects our soul and our heart from the arrows of the enemy. Righteousness or justice was for the philosophers the main virtue. It is this virtue which measures all the other virtues, wisdom, prudence, and courage. It is righteousness which guides man to do all of his duties well and to lead a harmonious life. Only with a life of personal and social justice can we fight for Christ and be the light and the salt of the earth, as He asked us to be. When justice is missing, then the salt loses its quality of saltiness; it loses its value and the world ignores it.

The whole world seeks truth and justice. Both have been found in their perfect state in Christ. And we must live with these two virtues if we are to stand upright in our spiritual struggle. We must do this not only as individual persons but also as the Church and the world. If we do not live with the truth and with righteousness, then we have already lost the battle even before we have begun to fight.

D. OUR CHRISTIAN LIFE

Peace. "Having Shod Your Feet With the Equipment of the Gospel of Peace."

(Eph. 6:15)

For a soldier to fight he must have the proper equipment on his feet or he cannot stand firmly. The best equipment for a Christian in this regard is "the gospel of peace." Our gospel is Christ Himself who is our peace. With His sacrifice, He destroyed the wall of enmity and brought us peace, peace with God, and peace among men. Christ made us all into one new man, one building, one body, one temple of God in the Holy Spirit (1 Cor. 12:12-13; Eph. 2:13-22; 4:4). When we know the Gospel well and receive Christ, our peace, into our hearts and minds, then we can run freely and spread the peace of Christ everywhere in our surrounding world. And this is our most important mission in the world. "Blessed are the peacemakers, for they shall be called sons of God." "As it is written, 'How beautiful are the feet of those who preach good news of peace and salvation!'" (Mt. 5:9; 28,18-20; Rom. 10:15; Is. 52:7). And yet for us to transmit this peace of the Gospel and of Christ we ourselves must acquire it first. We can give to others what we have ourselves (Acts. 3:6). May the peace of God fill and guard our hearts and our minds (Phil. 4:7).

Faith. "Besides All These, Taking the Shield of Faith."
(Eph. 6:16)

The most important part of our spiritual armor is "the shield of faith." Living faith contains in itself truth, righteousness, and peace. Faith is like a great shield that protects the entire body of the soldier at the time of battle. A living faith is a great shield that protects the entire person of the believer, and on this shield of a strong faith, "all the flaming darts of the evil one" are broken and quenched. All temptations, both internal and external, are repelled by faith and they cannot affect the heart and the integrity of the character of the believer. Temptations will always be there, but faith, like a sacred shield, will protect us. When faith is shaken within us and doubts control us, then everything in our life is shaken and insecure, no matter how strong we may otherwise be. Let us have a deeper knowledge of our faith, and in order to keep our faith alive let us pray: "Lord, give us more faith." "And lead us not into temptation, but deliver us from evil."

Salvation. "Take the Helmet of Salvation."
(Eph. 6:17a)

The helmet is to protect the head of the soldier. The helmet for the Christian is the certainty of our salvation in Christ, the assurance of our salvation. Salvation is given to

D. OUR CHRISTIAN LIFE

us freely in Christ, and we accept it in faith and thanksgiving. Faith in the reality of salvation is the personal experience which the believer has of the love of God, of the forgiveness of sins, and above all of the certain hope for the completion of salvation: the resurrection of the dead and the eternal life near Christ, when we shall "always be with the Lord" (1 Thess. 4:16-17; Jn. 17:24). "I await for the resurrection of the dead and the life of the age to come." All of these constitute the spiritual helmet that protects our mind and our thoughts from evil imaginations and doubts. All of the saints made tremendous efforts to protect the mind from evil thoughts or even from thoughts that are not related to our salvation. Their only thought was Christ and our salvation in Him. When we are certain of our salvation in Christ, when we feel within us the love of God in Christ, then we can protect ourselves from the many attacks we suffer today, both from without and from within. This is why it is necessary to strengthen our faith with love, with study, and with personal and corporate prayer. Our faith is especially reinforced in the Divine Liturgy where all of us together, as one people of God, as the one saved community, confess and affirm faith in our salvation and receive Christ within us unto remission of sins and life eternal. In the Divine Liturgy, every other thought disappears. All together we live our salvation; we thank and glorify God for His love and we live with the joy of faith here and with the hope of eternity: "May the name of the Lord be blessed now and forever and to the ages of ages." Without hope for a future one cannot speak of religion. Let us take the matter of our salvation in Christ seriously.

The Word of God. "The Sword of the Spirit." (Eph. 6:17b)

The "sword of the Spirit" is the word of God. The Gospel which the Church teaches is the word of God which calls us to reconciliation and salvation. And Christ is the Λόγος (Logos-Word) of God as a Person. The word of God is always creative. With the words, "Let there be," God created the world. And Christ is the Logos of God, the power of God, and the wisdom of God for the recreation of the world (Rom. 1:16-17; 1 Cor. 1:23- 24). The word of God, the Gospel, when we hear it and study it with faith and prayer, is a spiritual weapon in the hands of the Christian soldier to fight and to overcome temptations, sin, evil, and the enemies of the truth. It is a sharp two-edged sword that examines the depths of the soul, judges and condemns evil thoughts, and calls to repentance and salvation (cf. Jn. 16:8; Heb. 4:12; 1 Cor. 14:25). The word of God is the only offensive weapon of the Christian. With the word of God Christ and the people of the Church defeat the enemies of the truth (Rev. 12:11; 19:21).

Without the Gospel as a guide in our life and as power within us, we cannot fight against and defeat temptations. Let us study and know well the word of God, i.e. know well Christ

D. OUR CHRISTIAN LIFE

the Word of God as the Church has learned and lives Him. Let us also transmit the word of God to the world around us, for it is truly a powerful weapon, the very wisdom and power of God unto salvation for us and for the whole world.

Prayer. "Pray at All Times in the Spirit." (Eph. 6:18a)

Finally, in the complete armor of the believer comes prayer, which is the greatest and most powerful weapon of the Christian in the spiritual struggle. Regular prayer, conscientious prayer, and prayer that is persistent and fervent is absolutely essential. Prayer with all and for all, prayer for the whole Church and for the whole world cannot be neglected. The whole Church, as St. Paul sees it, is the one army of God and of Christ fighting for the kingdom of God. Its battle is not against flesh and blood, but against the hostile spiritual powers. And to be able to stand upright and to succeed in its purpose, the Church must always be armed and ready with continual prayer. The work of the Church is a work of God, of Christ, and the Church must always be in constant communion with God the King, receiving directions, power, and protection from Him. The entire armor described above is possible only when the soldier is in close contact with Christ the leader when he feels Him being constantly by his side in the battle, "until the end of the world." And Christ will be by his side in every type of prayer: doxology, thanksgiving, supplication.

Ceaseless Prayer. "Pray at All Times."
(Eph. 6:18b)

As communication with God, prayer must be active at all times. "Pray without ceasing" and not only at a time of need (1 Thess. 5:17; Phil. 4:6). The entire life of the believer must be an ongoing prayer, a life that is spent in the presence of God and in communion with God, regardless of what the Christian is doing at any given moment. For this reason, the Fathers discovered and developed the unceasing prayer of the heart with these words: "Lord Jesus Christ, have mercy upon me a sinner."

Prayer in the Spirit. "In the Spirit."
(Eph. 6:18a)

There are many different types of prayer. But all of them must be "in the Spirit" (Rom. 8:16-26). Prayer is conversation and "communion" with God, and no one can stand before God and speak to God alone. We need the presence of the Holy Spirit, the Paraclete. It is the Holy Spirit that creates the atmosphere of prayer. Without the presence of the Holy Spirit, we do not know how and for what to pray. First, God the Father comes to us and we in the Spirit respond to His presence, and thus a dialogue of prayer begins. The Holy Spirit is praying with our spirit. This is the essence of every prayer. Man feels that he is in the presence of God, in the love of God, and he places himself and his problems in the hands of God, in His

D. OUR CHRISTIAN LIFE

love. In this spiritual state, we know for what things to pray and in what manner to ask for them. Then indeed we have "committed ourselves and one another and our whole life to Christ our God."

Prayer for the Saints and Faithful. "Making Supplication for All the saints."

(Eph. 6:18b)

Prayer is done for all the saints, that is, for all the faithful. The prayer of the Church is a common prayer and no one can be left out. The Church is the one people of God, the one army of Christ. We are all the one divine family and all together we pray for all to the Father. We pray for the others, and the others pray for us, as Christ prayed for all of us upon the Cross. The Christian who believes in the crucified Christ does not live only for himself. As faithful individuals, we pray for our personal needs, but we always pray for others as members of the one Church of Christ. When we truly pray for the other, then we are truly praying. When we can pray for our enemies we reach the likeness of Christ. For this reason, public worship is the most particular characteristic of the Church. The life of the Church is a symphony of doxology and prayer to God.

Prayer for the Servant of the Gospel. "also for me."
(Eph. 6:19a)

In the end, St. Paul asks for a particular prayer for himself, or rather for the Gospel, since he lives for the Gospel and for Christ and His Church. At the time of writing the Letter to the Ephesians, St. Paul was in prison, an ambassador for Christ "in chains." But the Gospel must be preached even in prison, and St. Paul is asking for a special prayer that he may be given utterance, inspiration, and power to proclaim the Gospel boldly and effectively. Prayer in the Spirit by the faithful gives utterance to St. Paul, but also opens the hearts of the hearers to receive the Gospel as the "word of God," to believe and to be saved.

The Gospel is power unto salvation, but without the inspiration of the Holy Spirit the Gospel is powerless to bring about the fruits that it should. The preaching ministry of the Church is a sacred act of ministry that has the power to save and sanctify, just as the Divine Liturgy is a commemorative kerygma that brings before us, with sacred rites, the one sacrifice of Christ and invites us to be raised up to the kingdom of God and to partake of it unto remission of sins and eternal life (1 Cor. 4:15; 11:26; Rom. 1:16; 15:16). This is why in order to be preached effectively the word needs the prayer of the Church. With our prayer for the preachers of the word of God, we all become apostles, ambassadors, and communicators of the Gospel, coworkers, and fellow soldiers in the saving work of Christ and the Church (Rom. 15:30; 1 Cor. 9:23).

D. OUR CHRISTIAN LIFE

The work of salvation is indeed the work of God in cooperation with man. And the power of the common prayer is indeed great. Therefore, "confess your sins to one another and pray for one another that you may be healed" (Jas. 5:13-18).

4. The Church in its Spiritual Struggle

The exhortation for prayer is the most beautiful image that St. Paul could have given us for the Church, for the meaning, the unity, and the purpose of the Church. The Church is the army of Christ. The work of the Church is a sacred one, the salvation of the world. We are all soldiers of Christ and we must be armed with the complete armor of God. Altogether, we must stand next to each other with Christ as our leader. We have but one purpose, to overcome "the world," to win the world for Christ, for heaven, "that God may be everything to all." In the Church, there can never be divisions into separate groups or individual persons. Divisions and separations break the solidarity of the front and the battle is lost. Neither can there be neutrality or desertion in the battle. Either we are with Christ or we are with anti-Christ (1 Jn. 2:18). Every division is a betrayal of the Church, a division of the indivisible Christ who became man for the Church (1 Cor. 1:13; Jn. 19:23).

The Letter of St. Paul to the Ephesians ends with his prayer for peace, love, and faith, the main elements of a life in Christ, which he extends to the faithful of Ephesus. The question is: Do we all understand this unity of the Church and our responsibility for its work? Do we have a sense of this unity particularly in our common prayer at the Divine Liturgy which is the prayer of the Church par excellence? Every laxity in the regular churching of the faithful and in prayer in the Spirit weakens the battle lines of the militant Church, allowing many wolves to enter the flock, often disguised as sheep, thus harming not only the lax members but the whole Church.

Today we do not believe so much in sinful temptations. We have presumably matured spiritually. We believe in science, in knowledge, and in the secular abilities of man, while our spiritual struggle has weakened and become lax. This is why we often fall into the trap of temptations, individuals, families, and entire societies. To fall is human. But to fall and to remain there in our fallen state and to consider this fall as the rule of life is not at all complimentary to man. After all, our life today is not all that attractive and desirable, in spite of the scientific progress and economic well-being we have achieved. Life is a struggle. Everyone is developing strategic plans, philosophers, psychologists, and politicians. Everyone is trying to arm himself more heavily today, and yet we do not really win any of these battles. The reason for this is that we do not have the right armor of God. The man of the twentieth century A. D. is the same, with the same spiritual

D. OUR CHRISTIAN LIFE

needs as the man of the first century A.D. And it is only with the proper armor of God, as St. Paul has described it for us, that is with faith, vigilance, prayer, and with a life in Christ, that we can create a new society of love, peace, and righteousness that will be desired by all.

The Truth

Because St. Paul presents to us the truth as the first spiritual weapon, it would be helpful to add here some additional thoughts on this important subject of truth. The truth is something that rational man will always seek. Every sincere person wants to know the truth, to witness to the truth, and to live by the truth. Without truth, man is in the dark. This is why scientists and philosophers passionately seek the truth, even though no one can say that he has found the whole truth. In fact, some people even doubt that there is such a thing as truth (Jn. 18:38). Yet truth does exist and this is why we seek to find it. But it is difficult to find it. We must seek truth willfully, with patience, and persistence, as Socrates used to say to the Sophists of his time who had doubts about the truth. Parmenides, moved by the uncertainty of the transitory world, began to doubt the very reality of the perceptible world. He needed to see a revelation, to be assured that the world truly existed, and therefore that truth also existed.

Plato taught that truth and the true is that which corresponds to reality, to true being, the being that truly exists. The true world is the intelligible world of ideas, the world of reality that exists "in a certain intelligible place," behind and above the world of phenomena, discernible only by the eye of the mind. The visible world is only a world of images and shadows which help us to think about the real world in its perfection. Visible things exist and have truth inasmuch as they partake of the ideas, the true reality. Thus the knowledge of visible things does not give us the whole truth; it gives us only certain "opinions" of men, which together with some truth contain also a great deal of falsehood.

Indeed the truth that corresponds to reality is undoubtedly very great and it is with great difficulty that we find it. It begins with a small speck of earth and reaches up to heaven, to God Himself who is absolute reality and absolute truth. If we do not reach this point, to know our God, we cannot say that we know the truth, we only have opinions and are still searching.

For faith, truth has a moral and religious character. Truth is identified with God who is the absolute reality. Furthermore, true reality for man is God and man, and man's relationship to God and to the world. Only God says, "I am." All other beings have existence and truth by participation in the life of God, the source of every existence and every life. "For from him and through him and to him are all things" (Rom. 11:36).

Christ and Truth

God is the ultimate truth. And we know Him only to the extent that He is revealed to us; to the extent that He comes to us in a personal relationship. All creatures speak to us about God, the Creative Mind that governs the universe. But above

D. OUR CHRISTIAN LIFE

all, God was revealed and came into communion with man in the Person of Christ. Christ, the Son and Logos of God, not only spoke to us about God and man and the world, but in His Person, we saw who God is as the Father of love. Without Christ, one cannot speak seriously about God, man, and the world. "No one has ever seen God; the only Son, who is in the bosom of the Father, he has made him known" (Jn. 1:18). In the Person of Christ, with His Cross, the Resurrection, and Pentecost, all the questions about God, man, and the world are illumined. In Christ we have seen what man is and the meaning of the world and of life itself. This is why Christ can say: "I am the way and the truth and the life... I am the light of the world... I am the living water and the bread of life... I am the resurrection and the life" (Jn. 4:10; 7:32-39; 6:35; 8:12; 14:6; 11:25; 18:37). In the Person of Christ "are hid all treasures of wisdom and knowledge..." and our life is hidden with Him in God (Col. 2:3; 3:2-4). This is why the knowledge of Christ is the most important knowledge that man can have. It is this knowledge that brings salvation and life (Jn. 8:30-32; 17:3; Phil. 3:7-11; 1 Cor. 1:24).

The Spirit of Truth

Christ is the truth, but it is the Holy Spirit, the Spirit of Truth, who abides in the Church until the end of time, that guides us to the fullness of truth about Christ and God, man, and the world. We cannot know Christ and God without the enlightenment of the Holy Spirit. The Holy Spirit speaks about the love of God in Christ; He calls the world to repentance, faith, and union with Christ; and thus the kingdom of God is built upon earth as it is in heaven. This is the purpose, the goal of the world, to become the perfect kingdom of God.

For Christian faith truth is not simply rational, philosophical knowledge and scientific achievement. It is knowledge of the very Person of Christ. We need to know Christ Himself and not something about Christ. Christ, Himself is truth itself. The truth in the Person of Christ is known as a personal relationship and communion with Christ in a mutual love, for a person is known only in a personal relationship. The more one loves Christ the more one comes to know Him and God, or rather, the more one experiences the fact that God acknowledges him or her as His beloved son or daughter. God is love and can be known through our love for Him. This is the love that casts out every fear (1 Cor. 8:3; Gal. 4:9; 1 Jn. 4:18). This is how the Apostles came to know Christ, with personal knowledge. And this is how the Church lives Christ in the Holy Spirit, with faith, worship, and life in Christ. The Church is called "the pillar and bulwark of the truth" (1 Tim. 3:16), precisely because it knows Christ the Truth. In the Church the believer knows the truth in a personal communion with Christ; he lives in the truth, is in the truth, and is born of God unto eternal life (1 Jn. 2:21; 3:13; Jn. 1:13; 4:24; 18:37; Eph. 4:25).

D. OUR CHRISTIAN LIFE

Outside of the life of faith of the Church man cannot come to know the truth in all of its wealth. Man misses the mark of truth, and cannot live the fullness of truth (2 Tim. 2:18-25). In fact, we could say with Plato that all the truths outside of Christ are mere "opinions," incomplete truths which have within themselves much falsehood and imperfection. All the truths of the world are partial and changing, but the truth of Christ covers everything: God, the world, man, salvation, eternity, and it remains to the end of time (Mt. 24:35; 1 Cor. 13:12).

Truth is ultimate reality, and reality is life, not intellectual knowledge. Truth is religious experience of the presence of God acting in Christ for the salvation of His world. This is truth for the Christian faith: the Person of Christ, as revealed in the mystery of the divine plan of salvation for mankind and the world. The truth in Christ is a mystery beyond reason, but when received in faith it clarifies all the mysteries which human reason leaves unexplained about God, man, and the world.

What About Science and Philosophy?

True science and true theology can never come into conflict in their search for truth. Science and philosophy seek to find the truth as best as they can in their investigation and study of the physical world. Christian truth is not a result of human science; it is truth received by divine revelation, an experience of a world-God relationship. Christian faith takes the visible world for granted and examines "the invisible" things of the world, the beginning of the world, the God who made the first "big bang" of the scientists, its relationship to God, and its final destiny in God. Science has its limitations, and where it stops faith takes over. While science cannot alone enter the realm and the subject matter of faith, Christian truth can illuminate the free work of science and provide for it some directions for thought and research.

The Truth of Christ and Man's Freedom

Man loves the truth because the truth liberates him from the darkness of ignorance and fear. Truth that does not liberate is not truth. Truth and freedom are God-given gifts. In the physical world, only man was created in the image of God and with the gift of free will. The gift of free will distinguishes man from all the other creatures of God and gives him a personality. It is only man with his ability to reason who can freely regulate his life, always within the given circumstances of life and the society in which he lives. The abuse of this freedom is an affront to the personality of man. Only sin destroys our true freedom.

Our freedom is and must be controlled by love and absolute respect for the freedom of other people (1 Cor. 9:19; 10:23), and by the will of God who only guides us and helps us to reach our true freedom in a life according to true human nature and God's real plan for man.

D. OUR CHRISTIAN LIFE

Man's freedom is of a dual nature: it is natural or political freedom and an internal or spiritual freedom. Both freedoms, gifts of God, are essential to man in order for him to live in dignity. Christian faith regards both freedoms highly. But particular emphasis is given to the inner, the spiritual freedom precisely because it is mainly this particular freedom that fashions the personal character of man. There are slaves who are free spiritually, and there are kings who live as slaves. When man is spiritually free, in control, and master of his life and not a slave of his weaknesses, then he can also live as a free citizen within a free society and contribute to the progress and common good of the community.

It is this spiritual freedom that Christ came to bring to us, freedom from ignorance, freedom from the passions, and freedom from the fear of death. This is why Christ says to us: "I am the way, the truth, and the life..." "You will know the truth, and the truth will make you free..." "If the Son has made you free you are indeed free" (Jn. 14:6; 8:32).

Only with the truth of Christ can man live freely, for only in Christ we have the full truth of God and man and the full meaning of life and the world. Without Christ, we remain in darkness, in the slavery of our weaknesses, no matter how many scientific truths we acquire. St. Paul who speaks out of personal experience about freedom sees the life before Christ, without Christ, as a life of slavery, slavery under the burden of ignorance and the passions, under the presence of external laws.

Even the Mosaic Law, as an external force, did not have the power to change us from within, spiritually, and to give us true morality and spiritual freedom. Many times the law, as an external force, pushes us even more toward evil. St. Paul describes this kind of slavery in his Letter to the Romans, especially his cry at the conclusion of the passage: "Wretched man that I am! Who will deliver me from this body of death? Thanks be to God through Jesus Christ our Lord! (Rom. 7:24-25). Christ redeemed us from the curse of the law (Gal. 3:13; 4:4-7).

Without Christ, then, and far from God, man lives alone, self-exiled, a stranger and a slave in this transitory world. Christ as "grace and truth" has liberated us from the burden of ignorance and the fear of death which had kept us down and has given us the spiritual freedom of the sons of God. He has brought us into the love of God where we, as His beloved children, cry out to Him, "Father" and experience the full wealth of life.

This is the real truth and the real freedom of man. This is the song of the saved Apostle Paul: "Thanks be to God through Jesus Christ." Christ has redeemed us from the curse of the law, of sin, and of death, and has granted us divine sonship. "So through God, you are no longer a slave but a son, and if a son then an heir" (Gal. 4:4-7; Rom. 8:16) of the glory of God through Jesus Christ. "For freedom has Christ set us free;" stand fast therefore and do not submit again to a yoke of slavery (Gal. 5:1-13).

D. OUR CHRISTIAN LIFE

Freedom and the Lay of the Spirit in Our Life in Christ

As children of God Christians are not absolutely free. Absolute freedom leads again to the slavery of the passions. This is why St. Paul emphasizes: "All things are lawful for me, but not all things are helpful... I will not be enslaved by anything" (1 Cor. 6:12; 10:23). The free children of God have the law of the Spirit, the law of Christ, and the law of love which is the fulfillment of the law. All of the laws are written in our hearts like a golden and royal law of love (Mt. 7:12; Jas. 2:8). Only the person who loves in Christ is truly free. He thinks and acts freely and spontaneously. He loves and does the good simply because it is good. He lives freely and comfortably as a child of God, in the nearness of God and Christ, and this is true freedom. Christ has liberated us out of love and He wants us to work for each other in love, building up the kingdom of the love of God (1 Cor. 9:19; Gal. 5:13). Love for God and for our neighbor is the essence of all the laws and of the prophets (Mt. 22:37-40; 1 Cor. 13:1-13). The very life of eternity will be a life of love.

Freedom truly is a great gift of God to man. We can say that the purpose of our life is to be liberated from some slavery, some external or internal distress that pressures our life. Perfect freedom can only exist and flourish in the truth of Christ. "And this is eternal life, that they know thee the only true God, and Jesus Christ whom thou has sent" (Jn. 8:32-36; 17:3).

Truth and freedom are gifts of God to man. They are tender flowers in our hands, and we must be very careful not to destroy them with our egotism and our selfishness. Both of these gifts are divine and we must approach them with faith and love, with respect and humility. Without faith, the God of love truth cannot be approached, and man cannot be liberated. Faith and the life of truth, as the Church lives it, leads us to freedom as sons and daughters of God and to eternal life, when we shall always be with the Lord, seeing His glory. This is the end the whole world anticipates (Rom. 8:18-25; Jn. 17:24; 1 Thess. 4:17).

E. THE HOLINESS OF MAN

1. Introduction

"Be ye holy for I am holy" (1 Pet. 1:16)

The main purpose in the life of man is to become holy, to be sanctified by God and to acquire the quality of holiness. Holiness is the positive side of our salvation in Christ. Our forgiveness and reconciliation with God in Christ is the first step. After we have been forgiven and reconciled, we can begin to grow in the Spirit of God toward holiness and theosis. Holiness or theosis is the final goal of man's life. From the beginning man was created in the image of God, and he was destined to reach the likeness of God. Man received the breath of God into his being, and he lives by his communion with God. This is what distinguishes man from all the other creatures. To live in a personal relationship and communion with God, who is absolutely holy, man must himself become holy; he must attain to the divine likeness.

What Is Holiness?

Essentially, only God is holy. God is the Holy One. It is the absolute holiness of God that makes us bow down to worship Him and not His omnipotence. Every thing and every person that is separated from the world and is dedicated to God, to serve the will of God, is sacred and holy. A man is holy when he is completely dedicated to God, living in God, through God and for God (Rom. 11:36; Gal. 2:20). Only Christ as man gave Himself completely to God. He became obedient to the will of God unto death, death upon a cross (Phil. 2:6-11). This is why Christ is the only Holy One, and we become holy through our mystical union with Him.

The Fall

Through the deception of the devil, man lost his direction toward God, and fell from his original glory. He turned his attention to the world to secure his life, contrary to the will of God. The corruptible world, however, cannot give true life to the spiritual man. "Man does not live by bread alone" but by his communion with God. Separated from God, the spiritual man "is dying of hunger" (Lk. 15:17). The mystery of the divine plan of God to save man through Christ begins here.

E. THE HOLINESS OF MAN

2. *Holiness in Christ*

The Son and Logos of God, the only Holy One, became man to bring man again to the way of holiness, to God Himself. This was the prayer of Christ to the Father on the night before the Crucifixion. "Holy Father, keep them in thy name... Sanctify them in the truth; thy word is truth... And for their sake I consecrate myself, that they also may be consecrated in truth" (Jn. 17:11-19). Christ is consecrated and is offered to God as a sacrifice for us to be sanctified. This is the depth of the mystery of Christ. He died in obedience upon the Cross out of love so that we may be justified, and become holy. In a sense, we may say that Christ lent us his sanctity. Christians are holy in Christ (1 Cor. 1:30; 2 Cor. 5:19-21; Eph. 5:25-27; Rom. 6:22-23). This is how the Apostles lived the mystery of Christ, and this is how the Fathers of the Church lived it also and expressed it in doctrines and in worship. In Christ, God became man, Theanthropos, to help man reach the divine likeness, to become holy, a theanthropos like Christ, a divine person by grace. With the Incarnation, the Logos of God received our human nature and in His Person He sanctified it and deified it, and together with it He sanctified potentially the whole of human nature. With the sanctified human nature of Christ as a sort of leaven, God recreates, refashions, and recapitulates the fallen world.

Human nature is one and indivisible; divine nature is also one and indivisible. Our natural relationship with Adam has caused us to inherit sin, corruption and death. Our spiritual, mystical union with the Incarnate Logos, opens the way for our holiness, for our union with God, for life and incorruptibility. Salvation and life is man's participation in God through the Person of Christ. "Therefore, if any one is in Christ, he is a new creation; the old has passed away, behold, the new has come" (2 Cor. 5:17-21; Rev. 21:5).

3. In the Holy Spirit

Sanctification and salvation was enacted once for all time and for all of mankind through the Cross of Christ (Heb. 9:12-28; 10:10). Our holiness, however, is not something static; it is a progressive life continued in the Holy Spirit throughout history. Our salvation begins with Baptism and continues throughout our entire life. Throughout our life we are ever becoming that which we received in our Baptism; we are ever becoming holy. Our life is a journey to holiness, an ascent from earth to heaven, to God.

The work of sanctification is continued in the Church through the Holy Spirit. The Church is a workshop of holiness. The Holy Spirit completes the work of salvation and He guides us to faith in Christ and to the life in Christ. Christ is formed in us by the Holy Spirit. He unites us mystically with Christ and sanctifies us. The Holy Spirit makes us partakers of the holiness of Christ, communicants of the divine nature and life, sons and daughters of God, gods by grace (Jn. 1:12-13; Rom. 8:14-17; 2 Pet. 1:4; 1 Jn. 3:2-3).

E. THE HOLINESS OF MAN

4. Synergy, Personal Struggle

Essentially, holiness is a gift of God in Christ for the faithful. But it needs our own contribution and cooperation to be completed. We neither become holy by ourselves with our insufficient works nor does God make us holy without our will and our cooperation. God does not want us to be predetermined robots, nor "humanists," independent of divine grace. The spirit of independence from God is considered a hybris, an insult to God. And we have seen this in the progenitors, Adam and Eve, and we see it also in contemporary man.

The work of Christ is a movement against the evil that entered into the world and is contrary to nature. Christ conquered the "world" of evil with the Cross (Jn. 16:36) and now wants man to be His co-worker, to continue His work. The sanctified faithful must work personally to make the sanctification they received from Christ at their Baptism a personal possession, and to help with their life and their words for the sanctification of the world. They are all athletes and combatants in the battle of life. In our Baptism, we promise to fight against Satan. The prize will be received at the end (2 Tim. 4:7-8). Salvation is given as a gift by faith and Baptism, but we have to grow in holiness. Holiness is our goal. This is the meaning of the exhortations: "Be holy yourselves in all your conduct." "Strive for peace with all men, and for the holiness without which no one will see the Lord" (1 Pet. 1:15; Heb. 12:14). "We are becoming what we are" by baptism, that is, saints, the sanctified and holy people of God.

5. Stages in the Spiritual Ascent

The very first thing that man needs in his spiritual struggle is faith in God, and a life in accordance with the will of God. The rich young man who had everything in life, approached Jesus to ask Him what he must do to have "eternal life," for this is what Christ was teaching, true life. And Christ answered him: If you want to have (true) life "observe the commandments." The first step for our sanctification is to observe the commandments of God. They were given to us by God and they are the best guide for a peaceful and harmonious coexistence with our fellow men and for our relationship with God. Christ did not come to abolish, but to fulfill the law by His teaching and life.

The young man in the Gospel believed that he had observed the commandments, and yet he did not seem to be certain about his life. Therefore he asks: "What more do I lack?" What more do I need to do to have the quality of life that my soul desires? The commandments are from God and they are good, and they can give life, but they depend on our disposition, on how we keep those commandments. In the Sermon on the Mount, the Lord showed us what is the deeper spirit of the Mosaic Law. Every virtue must be practiced from the depths of our heart and for the glory of God, and not hypocritically, out of fear or selfish motives to acquire some reward (cf. Mt. 6:1-6, 16-18). Whatever the believer does he does because it is the will of God and he does it before God Himself and for His glory. Every other type of goodness is not beneficial and perhaps even harmful.

E. THE HOLINESS OF MAN

Love

The measure and motive for virtue is the sincere love as it is simply presented in the golden rule: "So whatever you wish that men would do to you, do so to them; for this is the law and the prophets" (Mt. 7:12). Love is not a matter of law. Love is divine; it is life itself, the very mode of existence of the Holy Trinity. Our love is a divine gift, an inherent drive in man given by God to offer and to receive love, or rather to give of himself and to create new life and new love. This is what we see in the life of the family which is the home of human love.

God who is love gives freely and creates life; He forgives and saves (Jn. 3:16). And He wants our love also to build the kingdom of love that He established on the love of Christ (Col. 1:13).

Mutual love and mutual indwelling of persons, of God and man, is the essence of faith and religion. Love is the greatest thing in life; it is God Himself, it is Christ. Love must be spontaneous and infinite as is the love of God for us, and whoever does not live with love "cannot win anything in life," and "he is nothing" as St. Paul says in his hymn to Christian love (1 Cor. 13:1-3). This kind of love for God and for man we have seen mainly in the life of the Saints of the Church.

Holiness and Love

Yet, holiness is something more than keeping the commandments. Salvation and holiness is the work of the love of

God in Christ. Christ loved us perfectly and He wants our love to be perfect also. He wants us to love Him more than our parents and relatives, more than we love our very own life (Mt. 10:37-39). This is what He asked of us at the Mystical Supper. "As the Father has loved me, so have I loved you; abide in my love... This is my commandment, that you love one another as I have loved you... He who loves me will be loved by my Father, and I will love him and manifest myself to him" (Jn. 15:9-12; 14:21). Love of God and our neighbor is the greatest gift in our life. Without love one gains nothing; without love one is nothing but "a clanging cymbal" that only disturbs his fellow human beings.

The Love of the Saints

This strong love for Christ made the saintly faithful into the Saints of the Church. The Saints felt deeply the love of Christ and they loved Christ far above every other person or thing. The saints of course also love people, but for the sake of Christ, to bring them to Christ, to save them (1 Cor. 9:22; 10:33). Love for Christ is indeed the main source and power for our spiritual ascent or progress toward holiness.

The Ascetics

This love was especially seen in the ascetic Fathers of the desert. They took literally the words of Christ, and "sold everything" for the sake of the love of Christ. Christ became

E. THE HOLINESS OF MAN

the great treasure and the precious pearl of their soul. They sacrificed all worldly possessions in order to gain Christ. The goal in their life was to become perfect, to become saints. They wanted to be able to see Christ, to be united mystically with Him, and to have life eternal. The Saints of all ages experience the work of salvation in Christ as a bride, and bridegroom spiritual love (Mt. 25:1-14; Rev. 19:10; 21:9). Christ left the heavens and came to earth to seek man. Man leaves the world to meet Christ. In that meeting with Christ, man finds himself as well as the true life. Such people feel like strangers here on earth, as sojourners and immigrants. They have no abiding city here on earth, but are always journeying from this earth to heaven, to Christ, to God (1 Pet. 2:11; Phil. 1:23; 3:20; Heb. 13:10), who is their abiding and eternal homeland.

Man is a mixture of spirit and matter. He has within himself the breath of God that urges him toward God. In God man experiences true life, authentic life, without questions and anxieties. Apart from God, there is only the non-being, the nihil from which God created us. Without God, everything in life is temporal and uncertain.

6. The Journey Toward Holiness

The holy Fathers say that there are three main stations in the journey toward holiness: repentance, catharsis, and perfection, or vision.

Repentance

The first thing we need in our spiritual life is repentance. Repentance is to come to ourselves, to recognize our sin and our weakness. Repentance is to feel how lost and starving we are far away from God the Father and to make the decision to change our mind and way of life. Repentance is to deny worldly things and to return to God, and with love and tears to ask God to forgive us and to help us to make a new beginning in our spiritual life. Without repentance and forgiveness, we cannot be released from our weaknesses and begin a new spiritual life (Lk. 15:11-24). "We are all weak and the only natural life appears to be the life of repentance" (Lk. 24:47).

Catharsis

After the diagnosis of sin and forgiveness comes the catharsis, the cleansing of the heart. Christ is seeking our heart. "My son give me your heart, and let your eyes observe my ways" (Prov. 23:26). But to approach the Holy God and to receive Christ in our heart, our heart must be pure and holy (Mt. 5:8; 15:19; Ps. 51:12-19). What is not clean cannot touch what is clean. Whatever we offer as a sacrifice to God must be pure, without blemish. And the heart must be pure, free from worldly desires and thoughts. We must love God "with all of our heart." A heart divided and partial to worldly possessions cannot approach Christ, and cannot come closer to Christ.

E. THE HOLINESS OF MAN

Without this catharsis of the heart, our meeting with Christ cannot take place; our union with Christ and our sanctification in the Holy Spirit cannot be realized.

Asceticism

This is why the saints make a special effort to maintain the heart pure from every thought and desire that keeps them apart from Christ. They call this struggle for purity νήψις (nepsis), a condition of sobriety of spirit, of vigilance over their heart and mind. Their only thought is Christ and salvation: how to be worthy to receive Christ, the Bridegroom, and to be with Him in the eternal kingdom of God. Their fervent prayer is "Maranatha - Our Lord, come;" "Come, Lord Jesus!" (1 Cor. 16:22-23; Rev. 22:17-20).

The struggle of the Saints to keep their heart pure is called "the unseen warfare," a fight against the invisible powers, which are working in this world and in our heart. In the Epistle to the Ephesians (6:10-20), St. Paul describes the enemies and the armor of God by which we can overcome them.

Fasting

Fasting is the practice of temperance and self-control to keep the spiritual person free and in control over earthly desires and carnal appetites. Without self-control, man is a slave of the passions. Fasting is not a limitation but a fulfillment of life. When fasting is done out of love and for the glory of God, it is a spiritual exercise that strengthens the will and frees man from earthly things. Fasting raises man to more sublime spheres; it brings him to heaven, to God, the source of life; fasting makes man angelic.

Prayer

Another important means of sanctification is prayer. Prayer is the main weapon in our spiritual struggle, and it is available to everyone. Prayer is direct communion and conversation with God. And the more we converse personally with God the more we know Him and love Him. No matter where the believer may be, he is before God, and the relationship to God is one of prayer and worship. And the life of the Saint is a life of prayer and worship. With mental prayer, or prayer of the heart: "Lord Jesus Christ, Son of God, have mercy upon me a sinner," the Saints can pray without ceasing no matter where they are. They can pray this prayer day and night and be in constant communion and conversation with God and Christ in the Holy Spirit. When does prayer stop? When the goal of prayer is achieved when one feels forgiven when the Saint has received the Holy Spirit when he feels himself in the presence of God and in His love. When this blessed state comes to the Saint, he does not need to speak in words anymore. He is now listening to God's will, in contemplation (1 Cor. 2:9-13; 2 Cor. 12:2-4). The hesychast saints (those who practice this sacred quietude of silence) can stand for hours before Christ and pray mentally in silence. They communicate mystically with God and delight in mys-

E. THE HOLINESS OF MAN

tical blessings. The prayers of the Saints in the desert are the greatest love and help that they offer for the world.

Απάθεια (Apatheia), Dispassion

With study, prayer, fasting, and vigilance over the passions, the sinful inclinations, and actions of the body and the soul, the Saints attain the state of απάθεια (apatheia), dispassion; they acquire the "likeness of God" and become similar to Christ who is the only dispassionate and sinless One. Apatheia is the perfection of the spiritual life of the Saint, the total victory over the passions, and the perfect dedication to Christ. The Saints reach a state of total immobility; evil and sin do not affect them or move them. The desires may be present, but they cannot affect the Saints who have died to the desires of the world (Rom. 6:6-18; Eph. 6:16; Gal. 5:24; 6:14). The Saints live only for God and Christ. Their life is a perpetual "memory of God" and of the presence of Christ. The saints cease to live in the world. They even forget their natural needs: food, drink and sleep. They live in prayer and communion with God. They live by the grace of God. In this state of apatheia, they find the perfect harmony and serenity, and peacefulness of the soul, which is what we usually lose with sin. Sin is a "disorderly movement of the soul" that disturbs the heart and troubles the mind, causing man to lose communion with God and spiritual peace and serenity.

Θέωσις (Theosis), Deification

This perfect state of holiness, this perfect communion of man with God is called Θέωσις (theosis), deification by the Fathers of the Church. This is the faith of the Church: In Christ, God became man so that man may become god by grace (St. Athanasios), a "partaker of divine nature" (2 Pet. 1:4). The difference between the created man and the uncreated God will remain forever. As for the essence of God, we cannot even think about it, for God is υπερούσιος (hyperousios), beyond essence itself. Ultimately, theosis means to be with God; to stand before God without fear of death (Ex. 33:12-23).

θεοφανισ (Theophanies), Divine Visions

In this state of perfection, the Saints see θεοφανις (theophanies), visions of God. Out of infinite love, the invisible God visits man in a perceptible manner; He reveals His glory and proclaims His will for the world. (cf. Abraham, Moses, Isaiah, the Apostles). The invisible and untreated God comes into contact with the created world through His creative and sanctifying energy. In His energies, God is light (Ps. 36:9; 1 Tim. 6:16; 1 Jn. 1:5) and He appears as light, as a flash of light that enlightens man, particularly in the heart. Man is always seeking the light and God is the only "true light that enlightens every man" (Jn. 1:9; 8:12). The vision of the light is a personal, existential, mystical experience of communication with God.

E. THE HOLINESS OF MAN

This divine light was seen primarily by the Apostles on Mt. Thabor. In the glorified face of Christ, they saw, through the power of the Holy Spirit, the glory of the Father (Mt. 17:5; Jn. 1:14).

The Uncreated Light

The light which the Apostles saw and which the Saints see even today is not something created, natural, sensible, and perceptible by everyone. It is an uncreated, natural energy or activity of God which comes toward us. It is the reflection of the glory of God coming to man. This light floods and permeates the whole personality of the Saint, making him also into light that can be perceived in his face.

The Vision of God

In a formless divine light, the Saint sees the glory of the invisible God. God is spirit and has no form. Rather, he sees the face of Christ, however dimly as in a mirror (1 Cor. 13:12). Christ is the natural image of God. In Christ, we have seen and continue to see God, His glory, and His love. In the Person of Christ, we see the whole mystery of the salvation of the world. This is how the Apostles saw Christ on Mt. Thabor. Christ the Savior is in the center. The prophets speak about the Passion of Christ. The cloud of light is the presence of God in the Holy Spirit. The voice of God the Father from within the cloud of light confirms what the prophets are saying about Christ (cf. Lk. 9:28-36; Rev. 5:5).

REFLECTIONS ON OUR ORTHODOX CHRSITIAN FAITH AND LIFE

In the Heart of Man

This light and the vision of the glory of God and the face of Christ become perceptible primarily in the heart of the Saint. Man is created as an image of God and only in man's pure heart can we see the image of the invisible God (Mt. 5:8). There in the enlightened heart, God speaks, and there the Saints come to know God and His will for the world.

This kind of knowledge transcends every perception and every thought. The Saints know God in a spiritual manner that transcends knowledge in the usual sense. They know God as if they have become known by God, as St. Paul would say (cf. 1 Cor. 8:3; 12:12; Gal. 4:9). Knowledge of God is not what I am thinking of Him, but what God thinks of me, and how He acts upon me in His love. God is not an object for examination and scrutiny to become known by us; God is the living and acting God. It is God who knows us and recognizes us and accepts us as worthy recipients of divine grace and salvation in Christ. The Saints see God as the incomprehensible Holy God. In a "super-ignorance" they have a "super-knowledge" of the "super-incomprehensible." This knowledge of faith is the most certain knowledge of God, precisely because it is a personal, an existential experience of the presence of God. The invisible and essentially inapproachable God comes out of His nature and enters into a personal relationship and communion with man. And thus man comes into communion with God. This communion and relation between God and man is the most

E. THE HOLINESS OF MAN

important element in faith. Man is united with God, lives in God, partakes of the life of God, even though we are unable to describe the life not only of the invisible God, but also of man created in the image of God. Both are deep mysteries (Jn. 14:20; 17:23).

There in the divine light, in the experience of the love of God, the deification of man is completed. The Saints partake of divine grace by sharing in God's divine energies; they are sanctified and transformed, becoming angel-like, Christ-like, God-like by grace. Living in the eternal love of God, they do not have a sense of a beginning or of an end; they become eternal as God desired and destined man to be.

Eschatological Visions

In this infinite love of God, the Saints transcend the natural and historical boundaries of life. They live and experience the present and the future, earth, and heaven, together. They see man as God created him to be, in the image of God, in all of his majesty in the present and with the gifts that He has prepared for him in the future, in eternity (1 Cor. 2:8-13).

This is the so-called θεωρία (theoria), the contemplation of the Fathers, a vision in the Holy Spirit. This is why they become the theologians and teachers who can teach us about God, man, the world, and eternity. This is how St. John the Evangelist teaches us about the life of the Church in its struggle in history and in its glory in the future age (Rev. 4:5, 21-22).

This, then, is deification or sanctification and this is the real salvation of man: to live in the presence of God in the Person of Christ and in the Holy Spirit and in the Church as the people of God.

7. Man is Between Heaven and Earth

Man is not simply the summit of all creation. He stands between heaven and earth. He is created as a link between the physical and the spiritual world. Man is not only a microcosm, he is also a microtheos, a god by grace. Man lives on earth, but is seeking heaven. He is an image of God, but desires the very archetype of that image. Man lives only to the extent that he knows and communicates with God; to the extent that he has God, who is life itself, in his own being. For Christian faith, knowledge and life is a spiritual experience of communion and participation in God (2 Pet. 1:4). And we know and communicate with God only to the extent that we experience spiritual progress; only to the extent that we become in the likeness of God in virtues, in goodness and righteousness, in holiness and love.

With the catharsis and the virtue of love, our heart will become a mirror in which one can see what God must be like in His goodness, but not, of course, in His essence. This is the pristine, but also the ultimate beauty of the soul of man: to reflect the beauty and the glory of God (Mt. 5:16). This reality

E. THE HOLINESS OF MAN

was revealed to us in its perfection in the Person of Christ (Jn. 14:8-11; 2 Cor. 3:18; Ex. 34:29-35). We too must be conformed to the image of Christ (Rom. 8:29). Know yourself well, and you will know God also.

We are God's children who resemble Him. The beauty of God's goodness, which we know to be within us and around us, attracts us toward heaven. The ascent toward heaven, however, is difficult and the distance between God and man is great. In Himself, God is inapproachable, and we will never be able in this imperfect world to reach a perfect communion with God. The life of the believer is a love journey of the soul for the heavenly Bridegroom, according to St. Gregory of Nyssa. We possess God only as much as we love Him, and the loved One purifies and deifies man and unites Himself to him (St. Gregory the Theologian, Oration 7).

The Perfect is Yet to Come in the Future

The Church experiences these spiritual realities here and now by faith, with virtue, with worship, and particularly in the Divine Liturgy. Indeed, in the Divine Liturgy heaven and earth, the present and the future, God and men become one. The angels, the saints and Christ together with us offer the eternal sacrifice of Christ as a thanksgiving and a doxology to God.

With Baptism we have all been saved, and yet the Holy Spirit is still working our sanctification in the Church of Christ. With Baptism, the faithful die to the desires of the world and are born into the new life; they become a "new creation," putting on Christ and living in the grace of God. With the Holy Eucharist, we are nourished spiritually and grow in holiness and deification. In the communion prayers, we say: "The body of God deifies me and nourishes me." This is especially true if all of us understand and feel deeply what is happening in worship, and are praying fervently and thanking God altogether from the depths of our soul, "with one mouth and one heart."

And yet the fullness, of perfection is to be experienced at the glorious Parousia of Christ. It is there in the future that we shall see Him "as he is," and we shall become similar to Him (1 Jn. 3:2; 1 Cor. 13:12). Here we have only the first fruits, the foretaste, of the Holy Spirit. We still need to run the race, to continue the spiritual struggle to acquire the perfection in heaven (Phil. 3:12-21; 2 Tim. 4:7-8; Heb. 12:1).

8. Conclusion

This is the life in Christ. A life of faith, love, and communion with God in Christ and the Holy Spirit. And the question is: Does this apply to all? Can we all reach this height of the Saints? And the answer is, Yes. Yes, this is the purpose of life for all. We are all the image of God and in the process of acquiring divine likeness, becoming "conformed to Christ." This is the reason why Christ became man and remains forever the model for us to follow Him. We are all

E. THE HOLINESS OF MAN

called to become holy. We all have to experience the new life in Christ and to strive for sanctification. We are all called to purify our heart, to be united with Christ, and to be with Him forever. Each one, however, will climb the steps toward perfection according to his or her own ability, according to the grace received from God and the role that he or she has been placed in the Church to serve (Rom. 12:3; 1 Cor. 12:11; Eph. 4:7).

God alone is holy in Himself. We become holy to the extent that we are freed from earthly things and with love dedicate ourselves and our families to God; to the extent that we allow Christ to live within us and the Holy Spirit to work our sanctification. What is needed from all of us is sincere faith, humility, and unbounded love and dedication to God. The love of God for us demands our love also for God and for our neighbor. And this we all can and must do, no matter in whatever position and condition we may live, as long as we have the will to do so. Our Saints have shown us the way to sanctification: faith, love, prayer, and ascetic self-control. Thus, with the grace of God, we too can become saints, models of Christian life, and light to the world, as Christ asked it of us. This is the purpose of life and this is our mission, both as individual persons and as the Church.

The vision of the uncreated light is a gift of God that is given to the few, to the giants of faith. And even they receive only a few rays, a few drops from the ocean of divine light, and for only a few brief moments. At the Judgment, we shall not be asked if we have performed miracles or if we have seen this uncreated light, but rather if we have shed tears of repentance and if we have shown love.

The Saints and Us

Let us not be jealous of the Saints. They are the elect, the heroes of our faith. They are our Saints, the gifts of God to the Church. We are all one family of God; we present the Saints to God; we project them in the life of the Church. We thank and glorify God for giving them to us. Moreover, we ask the Saints to pray for us. The whole Church is praying and glorifying God through Jesus Christ in the Holy Spirit. Now, the perfect we shall all see together in the glorious Parousia of Christ. Then "the Holy Spirit will enlighten all like a star, and Christ will be visible in our midst as a shining sun," according to St. Symeon the New Theologian (cf. Rev. 21:23; 22:5).

This is the mystery of our faith, the mystery of God, man, and our salvation in Christ. In Christ, God came personally into the world to save the world that He created. The Son and Logos of God became man and dwelt among us. He shared our pain and died upon the Cross so that we may be saved (2 Cor. 5:17-21). The salvation and sanctification of man will be also the salvation and sanctification of the whole world (Rom. 8:19-21).

This is what the Apostles saw in the Holy Spirit during the great theophany at the Transfiguration of Christ on Mt. Thabor, namely the mystery of our salvation in Christ. This is

E. THE HOLINESS OF MAN

also what they mainly wrote about in the Gospels, that Christ came to justify us and to give His life as a ransom for all (Mk. 10:45). This is also what the Saints see in the visions of the divine light. They see God in the Person of Christ who was crucified and resurrected for our salvation. These are the same spiritual realities that we experience in the Divine Liturgy, namely, the love of God in the sacrifice of Christ. United with Christ in the Holy Spirit we offer ourselves together with Christ to God the Father as a spiritual sacrifice of thanksgiving and doxology for our sanctification. This is what we shall see in a perfect way in the glorious Parousia of Christ: Christ as the sacrificed Lamb in His glory, in His marriage with the Bride, the Church, for an eternal life and kingdom (Rev. 5:6; 13:8; 19:7; 21:9; 22:5). In the glory of Christ, we shall always be seeing the glory of God the Father who shall be shedding His divine light upon us eternally (Rev. 21:23; 22:3-5).

Everything in the world is a mystery, and everything tells us that God exists and guides the world toward its goal. He does everything for us, and He wants us to follow Him, to freely work with Him to build the kingdom of God, the kingdom of eternal communion in faith and love.

The only thing God demands of us is to have faith in God and man; to have purpose in our life, to have love, mutual respect, and cooperation. This is what we all cherish and long for. And all of these are to be achieved only in the love of God in Christ. Christ is the way, the truth, and the life. Alone, by ourselves, we only manage to destroy ourselves. And we see this tragic situation enacted in our own times.

We need to know ourselves in Christ, and to set our hearts towards our sublime goal, with a firm orientation upward, to meet Christ and to enter the kingdom of God. Without such a goal and without such hope we cannot fight the good fight. The question is: How much do we love Christ? What place does He have in our heart? Is it the first place, the second, or the last? (Gal. 2:20).

The Saints have shown us the way with their very lives. And they invite us to follow them in our spiritual ascent. The way seems to be an upward struggle and the ascent difficult. The steps of this spiritual ascent are many, and their number may vary from person to person. The ladder for this divine ascent, however, has been placed in our heart by God Himself, so that we may ascend up to heaven, to God, to Christ. Every single step as we climb upward is an act and gift of God that gives us life and spiritual joy. May God truly grant to all of us the ability to understand and experience the height, the light, and the joy of life in Christ, a life near God. And with the grace of God may we ever be climbing with love the steps toward perfection and holiness. At the final step, at the summit, Christ, the divine love, waiting and calling us to Himself:

F. CONCLUDING QUESTIONS AND REFLECTIONS

1. *The Christian Faith as Religious Experience of Redemption*

All of Christian teaching is in essence an expression of the religious experience of salvation in Christ. Salvation was the main spiritual thirst of the New Testament times. John the Baptist, John, Peter, Andrew, Philip, Nathanael, and all the Apostles, were expecting the Messiah-Savior. "We have found the Messiah!" was their familiar expression, as they led each other to Christ (Jn. 1:29, 41-45; Lk. 2:10-14). The thirst for salvation guided the Rabbi Paul, who was persecuting the Christians, also to find Christ. Paul had heard about Christ from Stephen and other Christians whom he had been persecuting. Perhaps he had seen and heard Christ Himself when he was a student of Gamaliel. But he must have seen Him without a personal interest.

During the incident on the way to Damascus, Paul saw Christ for himself, for his own salvation, that is, existentially, as contemporary philosophers and theologians would say. In the Person of Christ, Paul saw the Messiah-Savior. And he saw this salvation in the Cross of Christ and in the Resurrection, for both of these go together. The light of the Resurrection illumines the scandal of the Cross.

Paul recognized Christ as the Savior-Redeemer of man from sin and death. This slavery of sin and the "curse of the law" troubled the educated rabbi much more than the Roman occupation of his country and the social problems of the times. For Paul, a Christian slave could live with more freedom than a king of that time.

Thus, the Paul who struggled to fulfill the works of the Law found salvation in faith, in the love of God which is in Christ (Rom. 3:24-25; 8:31-39; Eph. 2:8-10; Gal. 2:16). This salutary love of God enlightened the eyes of the soul of Paul, and the persecuting rabbi became the inspired Apostle, the ambassador of Christ to the nations. He came to know Christ as the great mystery of the love of God, hidden for ages in the eternal will of God (Eph. 3:8-12; Rom. 3:21-26; 2 Cor. 5:17-21). This is how Paul, saved in Christ, lived and taught and gave us the theological basis of the Christian faith. Truly, if someone is not interested existentially in his salvation, he cannot even know Christ, nor write about Christ with the power of St. Paul.

F. CONCLUDING QUESTIONS AND REFLECTIONS

What Did Paul Find in Christ?

Paul found in Christ the love of God for man, and this is salvation: knowing that someone loves you even with your shortcomings (Rom. 5:8; 8:35-39; Jn. 3:16).

Love and Christian Life

If love is to be perfect, it must be mutual; rich in giving and in receiving. Man receives love from God and responds with love through faith. Faith is the response of man to the love of God in Christ, and it is a love for God and for man whom God loved so much. This is how Paul sang the hymn of love which is an image of the love of God in Christ (1 Cor. 13).

Hope

Faith in the salvation accomplished in Christ also gives us the hope for another, higher, more divine life, sharing the glory of Christ (Rom. 5:2-5; Col. 1:5, 27; Tit. 3:7). Thus, Paul formulated for us the three great virtues which are basic and should distinguish the Christians of every age. "So faith, hope, love abide, these three; but the greatest of these is love" (1 Cor. 13:13). Faith, hope, and love is what that age desired, and these will abide as the philosophy and psychology of Christian faith and life. Religion is life, and it must be guided by a philosophy which gives meaning to life and support to the faith in the present and in the future. Man does not live in the present moment only, nor in the future alone. The present receives its meaning from the past, its root, but also from the future toward which it moves. Faith, hope, and love are upheld within the mystery of the love of God, who first loved us (1 Jn. 4:10; Jn. 3:16; Rom. 5:8). The Church offered Christ with the power of a life filled with faith, hope, and love, and with an opening to an infinite future. This is why every open heart received the Christian faith, and Christianity prevailed as a religious experience of redemption.

2. Perennial Questions of Christian Faith

For two thousand years, the Christian Faith has prevailed in the world as a universal religion of redemption. Christianity truly changed the known world of that time and continues to change the world, particularly the so-called western world, Europe and America. Christian and non-Christian people have recognized the spiritual height of the Christian truth, as the most humane teaching for mankind and society. And yet the mind of man has always brought forward certain questions for a rational understanding of the mystery of Christ, particularly when the life experience of the faith has been weakened.

The Person of Christ

The first question has to do with the Person of Christ. Christianity is not a religion that is simply dependent upon the teaching of Jesus Christ, as much as it is dependent upon the

F. CONCLUDING QUESTIONS AND REFLECTIONS

very Person of Christ. We do not only believe in the teaching of Jesus Christ, but we believe in Jesus Christ, as the Savior and the Lord of the world. This is truly the "great mystery" of our faith (1 Tim. 3:16).

The question was posed by Jesus Himself to His disciples, "But who do you say that I am?" (Mt. 16:15). This question cannot be answered by the human mind alone. Only in the Church which has the experience of salvation in the Holy Spirit can one know and believe and confess Jesus as the Christ, the Son of the living God, the Lord and Savior of the world (Mt. 16:16-17; Jn. 20:28; Rom. 10:9; 1 Cor. 12:3; Eph. 3:14-21; Phil. 2:11).

God-Man Relationship

Every religion presupposes a relationship between God and man, and the Christian religion understands the particular relationship between God and man as we have seen it in Jesus Christ, the Incarnate Word of God. This is a mystery, and the mind of man tends to complain: "This is a hard saying; who can listen to it?" (Jn. 6:60).

Some people have difficulty believing because Christ, they claim, has many extreme requirements. He asks for absolute faith in His name, and love beyond the love we have for parents and children and even our own life (Mk. 8:34-38). He asks that we confess Him as the only Lord and Savior of the world. Christ asks these things because His work is a work of God for the salvation of the world. Everything Christ asks of us is always for our benefit. He asks for faith and love because He first loved us and gave His life for our salvation (1 Jn. 4:10; Jn. 3:16). Our salvation and eternal life depend upon faith in the saving work of Christ and our absolute love for Him. Thus He taught us that the true life is a life of unlimited faith and love for God and mankind (Mt. 22:37-40; 5:43-48). Christ, moreover, asks us to confess Him as Lord of the world, because with His death Christ saved the world. "...One has died for all… that he might be lord both of the dead and of the living" (2 Cor. 5:14; Rom. 14:7-9; Phil. 2:6-11).

Mankind needs a leader, a Lord, and Christ is the only good king who rules with love and justice and grants life eternal (Mt. 11:27-30; Jn. 1:3-4; 17:2-3; Acts 2:36).

Free Will, Life, Earth, and Heaven

Certain liberal thinkers do not accept Christ because with His teaching, they claim, Christ constrains our life and deprives us of our free will. He does not allow man to regulate his life by himself. They also say that the Christian teaching is irrelevant to our life, to our age. It speaks about another life, a future life, and thus deprives us of the joy of the present life.

Free will is truly a gift from God, given to a free and rational man so that he can by himself direct his life, always within the laws of nature and social life. Everything in the world has its natural laws, provided by God, the law-giver. Christ did not

F. CONCLUDING QUESTIONS AND REFLECTIONS

come to constrain our life or our free will. Christ came "that they may have life, and have it abundantly" (Jn. 10:10). Christ does not compel man; He simply points us in the right direction. We must choose and decide to live the good life with our own free will. Christ simply teaches us how to live "with justice and peace and joy in the Holy Spirit" so that we may succeed in fulfilling the purpose of our life here on earth and also inherit the eternal and abiding life of heaven. With the remarkable invitation: "Whoever would come after me..." Jesus expressed the majesty of Christian freedom. Man however lives freely as long as he lives "naturally,", as God created him to live, with faith, love, and communion with God and his fellow human beings. All things are created for man and man is created for God.

Have we ever stopped to think seriously about what life is? Scientists are seeking to discover the initial synthesis of material elements that produced the first life. Yet they readily admit that life has something unique that is not related to matter. This uniqueness is "the source of life," that force which regulates all those complex combinations and keeps the various organisms alive. Life is a miracle in the physical world that remains a mystery in the mind of man.

The problem of the origin of life is one of the last major gaps to be filled in man's knowledge of total history. A definition of the phenomenon of life that is universally satisfactory is impossible. Life is a phenomenon in the universe, a movement that proceeds according to a purpose.

Man is in this flow of life; he participates in life without being able to completely describe it rationally. Faith knows that life is a gift from God the creator. God who is life itself and the source of life ordered that life come out of the physical matter. With a particular creative action, God fashioned man out of the earth. Whether we call this a special action of God or evolution, life remains a miracle and a mystery in the physical world, which presupposes a living God, whose name is "The Being," "He who is." "God created man in his own image, in the image of God he created him" (Gen. 1:27).

The life of man is even more mysterious, and it is the life of man that interests us because man alone thinks and asks questions, not the monkey or the lion.

The life of man, like every life, is a movement according to a purpose. We can say that man does not possess life, but rather that he is struggling (with food, with knowledge, particularly with society and other persons) to attain life, the perfection of which he is always seeing in some future. But death puts an end to this movement toward life. Therefore, one could say that human life is "a life to death."

For Christian faith, however, the life of man is a great gift of God for a great purpose. We enjoy this life here on earth in God, that is, according to the laws which God has provided for life. Through death, we end up in God who is

F. CONCLUDING QUESTIONS AND REFLECTIONS

the source of life. The created life of man is moving toward the uncreated life, toward God Himself. The image moves toward the archetype, toward the likeness of God, toward holiness, and deification.

Everything in the world moves according to a purpose during certain times and seasons. The earth rotates on its own axis and revolves around the sun for a period of one year. The universe also rotates in its own huge cycle within the hands of God. The spiritual man also moves throughout his entire life here on earth, only to flow out into the great cycle of eternity near Christ and God. Only in the eternity of God shall all find the fullness of life, the eternal, the true life. Here on earth, we have only limited cycles.

For Christian faith, life, earth, and heaven are intertwined into one. Everything constitutes the one world of God. Heaven is what we call symbolically the spiritual place where God and the spiritual beings are. But God is everywhere, in the universe and in our hearts, and He seeks to speak to us while we in turn speak to Him. Man's life is also one. It begins here and finds its fulfillment in heaven, in God, in holiness, in the likeness of God, in our union with God in the eternity of divine wisdom, and in the love of God in Christ (Rom. 8:31-39). Let us not deprive our life of the joy of hope in the eternal.

3. What in Reality Does Christ Ask of Us?

Christ asks of us to understand that we are not alone in life, in the world. We are beloved children of God. God wants us to live with love and respect for God, for ourselves, and for our fellow human beings. First of all, God wants us to respect ourselves and then the others as images of God. He wants us to hold ourselves high in the eyes of God and in the society in which we live. We are to demonstrate with our personal life what it means to be an image, a reflection of God. This is why God created us in His image, that we may be able to see in each other the face of God. In the pure heart of man, as in a spiritual mirror, we must be able to see the image of God. Christ is the perfect, natural image of God because He possesses the fullness of divinity (2 Cor. 3:18; Col. 1:15; Jn. 14:9).

All of the commandments regarding our relationship with our fellow human beings were summed up by Christ in the golden rule: "So whatever you wish that men would do to you, do so to them" (Mt. 7:12; Lk. 6:31). This means that no commandment is contrary to our true wishes or desires.

This is what Christ asks of us, and this is what we all ask for: to live in mutual love, to see the love of God around us and in our hearts, and to respond with our love to the love around us. We are "to stir up one another to love and good works" (Heb. 10:24). Christ wants us to be in a competition of love, seeking to be the first to love and help the other person. Every-

F. CONCLUDING QUESTIONS AND REFLECTIONS

thing must be done for the common good; each person must not think only of himself but for his neighbor (1 Cor. 10:24). The trouble is that too often we seek the love of others without offering our love and our help to anyone. This is where the frictions of life come into play. But Christ is not to be blamed for this, nor is religion. This is a result of the limited understanding that we have, regarding what man is and what life is according to God and our God-given nature. We forget that we are a diverse society of people, both adults and children, and that paradise was made for all the people together, not for individuals. Love one another as God loves us; love even your enemies. Be merciful even as your Father in heaven is merciful and kind to everyone. For then you become a son or daughter of the Most High, the highest achievement for man in life.

Sin

Christ only strikes out against sin. Sin is the abuse of freedom which eventually destroys both the freedom and the life of man. All the goods of the earth are given for man to enjoy as gifts from God, according to the divine laws for the improvement of the quality of life and the success of the purpose of each person in society. Life has a purpose and then works according to a purpose. Every deviation from this divine purpose, every abuse and wrong use of these goods becomes a sin, a missing of the mark of our purpose. Thus, life becomes unnatural and it leads us to the destruction of persons and societies. St. John Chrysostom says that sin is the only enemy of man, which destroys our life. Take sin out of our midst and everything is put right. Sin kills man because it separates him from God who is the main source of life (cf. Rom. 7:8-11).

What Does Christ Give Us?

What is the one positive thing that Christ has brought to us, and which is most important for mankind? In just one phrase, we can say that Christ has brought us the Truth. In the Person of Christ, we have the truth of God, of man, and of the world in its most perfected form. This is why Christ Himself is the Truth.

In Christ, we have the real "Know thyself," which is so very important to rational man. Only in Christ, from above, by revelation have we learned and seen what man truly is: the image of God, coming from God and returning to God (Rom. 11:36).

Faith, Hope, Love

Christ taught us that God is the Father of love, that we are all His children. The Fatherhood of God is the center of Christ's teaching. The main characteristic of the Christian teaching is faith in God the Father who provides for the birds and the flowers of the field, and much more for man who is created in His image. The whole life of Christ as man on earth was a life of faith, obedience, love, and regular communion with God the Father. All of this is given to us in the Lord's prayer, which is the briefest and most comprehensive

F. CONCLUDING QUESTIONS AND REFLECTIONS

and didactic prayer on the lips of every believer. Faith in the existence, presence, and love of God is a gift of God. God first reveals Himself as love, especially in Christ. We accept the love of God in Christ and respond with our own love. This is the faith that saves: our absolute trust in the love of God which is manifest in Christ. Without faith in God the Father, man is lost in the darkness of the mystery of the vast and indifferent world in which he lives, in spite of our many conquests and our progress in certain areas of knowledge.

Hope

With His teaching, His life, and especially with His Resurrection, Christ has reassured us that life does not end with death. Life is a journey toward perfection, for something better and more divine.

We do not live a life "that leads to death." We ought not to accept death as the purpose of life. The Christian accepts death as the end of this present life with the hope of another more perfect life. It is there, beyond death, that the purpose of life will be fulfilled, as the likeness to God, deification, a life of close communion with Christ and God the Father (1 Cor. 15:12-20; Phil. 1:23; Jn. 14:3; Rom. 8:35-39). Even the theory of evolution hopes for some better future, although it cannot define or determine it.

4. The Hope of the Resurrection of the Dead

Resurrection and eternal life is the heart of the Christian faith. "I expect the resurrection of the dead and the life of the age to come" is the confession of faith of the Church. The mind of man finds it difficult to think about resurrection and eternity, for both are outside the realm of the experience of creation, where our created mind functions. And yet without faith in eternity, we do not even understand the present things, for all exist within the infinite and eternal. Many persons of faith, virtue, prayer, love, and illumination of the Holy Spirit penetrated into eternity and believed in the eternity of the world in God. These were the prophets and the saints, and even certain philosophers. Emmanuel Kant was able to deny all the rational proofs about the existence of God because rational thought cannot penetrate the divine, but he was unable to deny the existence of God and the life of the soul in the hereafter. We all live in the realm of the infinite and eternal, in the divine: "In him we live and move and have our being" (Acts 17:28; Jn. 14:20-23). To experience, however, the eternal, we have to live a higher spiritual life. If we do not live here in a manner that is "worthy of our divine calling," if we do not live the eternal values of life, such as "righteousness and peace and joy in the Holy Spirit," then we do not dare to think about eternity in itself. The more we believe and live here on earth according to Christ, the more we experience and realize the eternity as a life in God, with all the blessings God has prepared for those who love Him (cf. 1 Cor. 2:9-13).

F. CONCLUDING QUESTIONS AND REFLECTIONS

New Creation and the Change of the Present World

Faith in the resurrection and the eternity presupposes a change in the present volatile world. Man asks himself: is it possible for the world to change? Both faith and science believe that the present world will change, even though we cannot prove the manner of that change. The world will change "as through fire" (1 Cor. 3:13-15; 2 Pet. 3:5-13; Rev. 20:9). Will the world change from the progressive warming of the elements of the world, or perhaps also from the fire of nuclear weapons that contemporary science has developed? This is not a question of faith. According to faith, there will be a "new creation," a recreation of the world. "We wait for new heavens and a new earth in which righteousness dwells" (1 Cor. 15:50-58; 2 Pet. 3:13; Rev. 21:1-6). For us, the world is one, and life is one. It began with God's word: "Let there be," in Genesis and it goes on toward perfection in the future. The beginning is from God, and the end is also from God. "Behold, I make all things new," says God from His heavenly throne (Rev. 21:5; Rom. 11:36).

There in heaven, we will have perfection. There we will have true knowledge of God, the world, and man. In heaven, we will see all things as they truly are (Rev. 21-22; 1 Cor. 2:9-10; 13:8-13).

5. Negative Questions

Many other people again have difficulty accepting the Christian faith because it teaches that only the Christians will be saved. And as concerned persons who care for humanity, they ask, "And what will become of the multitudes of non-Christians?" Every religion needs to believe in a better future for its adherents, otherwise, it is not a religion. All of us are struggling for a better life, and not simply to learn what hell is or is not. We cannot possibly know everything. Only God knows who is a believer and who is an unbeliever. Peter once asked Jesus about John: "Lord, what about this man?" And Jesus answered him: "...what is that to you? You follow me" (Jn. 21:21). This is what Jesus says to each one of us: You follow me, and you will have eternal life. "For man believes with his heart and so is justified, and he confesses with his lips and so is saved" (Rom. 10:9). We must be concerned with our own salvation, not what will happen to others. This is a matter for God who knows how to save His world. In any case, He does not save anyone without faith. Faith is the personal communion with God, and this is the essence of salvation, communion with God. In Christ, we have seen that God is Father who loves, and who wants us to follow Him so that we may abide always in His love (Jn. 3:16; 15:10).

Faith informs us that Christ, after the Cross, preached the Gospel, the good news of salvation, in Hades as well, to those who had died before Christ (1 Pet. 3:19). Will the opportuni-

F. CONCLUDING QUESTIONS AND REFLECTIONS

ty be given to those who did not hear the good news in their lifetime to hear it somehow? This also belongs to God, not to us. In any case, the Gospel of Christ, as faith and love, will be the basis for eternal life. We know that Christ is the personal invitation of God, who calls all to be reconciled and saved (2 Cor. 5:19-21; Lk. 19:10; Mt. 9:13). And those who accept the love of God in Christ believe that they are not lost but have life eternal.

Let us, therefore, not be lost in negative questions because they impede us from hearing the serious questions: "What do you say about Christ and your salvation?" We must of course hear the Gospel and believe. At the same time, we must acknowledge our weakness and our need to repent before we can expect to be saved (Mk. 4:11-12; Jn. 12:40). Let us know Christ and enjoy our life in Christ. Let our true Christian life present Christ to others so that they too may believe, and all of us can be "one flock," with "one shepherd." This is what Christ is asking of us. We must build on the structure of faith, and not destroy it with our negative questions and our doubts (1 Cor. 3:5-15).

6. The Name of God and the New Ideas of Each Age

Another question which creates a great deal of friction and division on matters of faith appeared in our own times. It is the question concerning the naming of God. Are we to refer to Him or to Her? When we theorize about God outside the realm of faith, the question seems rather rational, and timely. But if we think about it from the side of faith, this question is a rather daring one, even radical. The question is really too much! By reasoning like this man becomes the measure of God.

Faith is a life of personal relationship with God, and not a matter of theories about the name of God or the gender of God. When God dwells in our heart and we live according to the will of God, we do not ask what pronoun to use but rather we worship God and say: "May your name be great, O God!" When we lose our relationship with God, when God becomes something out there, then the questions arise. But these questions, without the faith, do not lead us anywhere but to doubt and disbelief.

Religion is life and life evolves. In its structure, religion uses expressions and symbols to live, express, and transmit its experience of the presence and communion with God in Christ and in the Holy Spirit. This is how the sacred tradition of the Church was developed, as life in the Holy Spirit. The Jewish and Christian revelation conceived God with the name symbol of "Father." The names of the Persons of the Holy Trinity do not refer to the essence or to the gender of God. They simply denote the distinction of the Persons and their relationship to each other within the one Divinity. The term Father means the head of the family, the provider, and protector, who is full of love for his wife, his children, his family, the Church. This is the

F. CONCLUDING QUESTIONS AND REFLECTIONS

term that Christ the redeemer used to speak to us about God. Christ came into the world as the love of God the Father. The God of the Christian faith is the Father of love. "Our Father," is our major prayer. Thus, the traditional term Father was sanctified and became a major element in the life of the Christian faith. In the fatherhood of God, we understand all of the love, the forgiveness, the salvation, the life which our soul yearns for, without ever asking if this term is correct or legal.

Those who believe and pray to God know what the term God the Father means to them. In no way whatsoever does the term Father ever mean domination of one gender over the other. This attitude would be most degrading for the God of love. As we have seen Him in Christ, God the Father is the Lord of our life, as the human father is the leader of the family. But this leadership does not mean despotism and arbitrary authority; it does mean love, sympathy, and protection, under the love of God the Father, God the Son, and God the Holy Spirit. This is of course the meaning of Father in the ideal Christian family.

This is how the sacred tradition of the Church developed. We can say that this tradition is the pathway of faith upon which the Saints of the Church have walked (Jude 3). By following the pathway opened up by the great men and women of the Church, we do not fear falling into the chaotic state created by unexamined human thoughts.

Modem man dares to ask the question: Is it right to keep for our age the term for God used by Sacred Scripture two thousand years ago? Our age has changed and the term Father can change to conform to the spirit of our times. But the question is: What is our age, and what is its spirit? Has man truly changed in his being and in his actual physical and spiritual needs? Moreover, has the eternal and immutable God changed? Has our relationship with God changed? Has the idea of the Father as protector and provider for the family changed? We are all one great family, the household of God. Is there anything good that we cannot find in the meaning of God the Father, as revealed to us by Christ? Certainly not! Why then do we need the change? The answer is: For our so-called modern times, an age of liberal expression in all things. Christ, however, would have given a different answer. He would have said: "Because of your little faith," at a time when mankind is radically divided in a struggle for predominance among whites-blacks, men-women, parents-children, rich-poor, etc. This, the experts tell us, is the result of the two great wars we lived through in this century. Our present age is therefore a war for equality. There is a war going on in the working place, in the athletic games, in the family life, and even in the life of the church. And now we even have a war for the name of God. Is it going to be He or She? And it is easy to find justifications: freedom of thought and expression in matters of faith; the motherhood of God can express more vividly the idea of the nurturing work of God. Primarily, however, we seem to be seeking to gratify our demand for equality, which is the spirit of our times. Who

F. CONCLUDING QUESTIONS AND REFLECTIONS

is going to have the right to establish the name of God? Thus we degrade the spiritual God to the level of human weaknesses. We relegate the uncreated God to the level of a creature and of an object for scrutiny; we lose completely the idea of God, the idea of the holy, the idea of sacred awe, which we need to feel in the presence of God. We do not speak of God anymore but of ourselves.

Unfortunately, the problem for equality between the sexes exists today. And the struggle will continue; laws are being enacted, even though such laws will not solve the problem satisfactorily for all. In fact, however, God, who has created all human beings in the image of God, has given equality to men and women. God has willed that man and woman be one. Two co-workers of God and not two opponents (Gen. 2:20-24). Only in God and with a life of cooperation with faith and love can the problem of equality be solved, or rather be prevented. But we must not seek to approach the questions of faith with thoughts and laws of a purely human nature. The God of faith is not an object of our rationality, much less an object of our emotions.

How Do We Speak About God?

First, we need to let our heart feel the presence of God acting and caring in the harmonious movement of the universe as a whole as well as in its smallest details. We must not take the beauty of the universe for granted. We know God only in His action and caring in the world and in our hearts. We feel Him as a Person speaking to our heart. God speaks to our heart, and only the heart can know God. The God of philosophical theories is not yet God. When we speak theoretically about God, we are simply playing with words and ideas about God; we do not believe in Him. This is nothing but "hybris," an insult to God as the ancients understood it. Once we grasp the idea of God as a caring Person, as our Father, our mind cannot play with words about the existence of God. Whatever we are able to say about God is a daring undertaking of our mind, for how can one speak about the infinite God who embraces everything, without being lost in sacred awe!

Our God is there, present, acting and caring as our Father and we can never dare to think of Him as being in a faraway corner of the vast universe, or even to see Him dead. We also know that we certainly are not God, for He alone is God.

"God is Spirit, and those who worship him must worship in spirit and truth" (Jn. 4:23). This is what Jesus said about faith in God. God is the Holy One, the wholly Other, the One who is beyond any created analogy or worldly designation. God is "anonymous" and "hyperonymous," without name and transcending any name. The Church says that God is infinite, uncircumscribed, and incomprehensible.

It is God who speaks about man, and not man about God. God speaks because He knows man, and man listens and obeys (1 Cor. 8:2-3; 1 Sam. 3:10). One approaches into the

F. CONCLUDING QUESTIONS AND REFLECTIONS

presence of God with a deep sense of sacred awe. We approach God as a Person, to meet Him, to get to know Him, to speak to Him; to have Him speak to us, and for us to listen to him; to become aware of His love, His grace, and to have our present and future life in Him. God does not force us to believe Him; He only invites us with His paternal love. If we freely and lovingly believe in Him, we listen to Him, worship Him, and we have life, peace, love, and hope for an eternal life in close communion with God in Jesus Christ and in the Holy Spirit.

Christ did not change the traditional terms of the Old Testament to correct the faith in God; He illumined, lived, and taught the meaning of the Law in all of its depth. The only thing that Jesus said is that we must worship God "in spirit and truth." And this is what we mainly need today: to know our faith in all its depth as the Church has lived it for two thousand years, to love and to worship God "in spirit and truth," and not to be conformed to the worldly conditions of today, but rather to be transformed spiritually (Rom. 12:1-2).

Many problems with which the Church is confronted today come from the efforts of certain persons who seek to understand the nature of God, Christ, and the Church rationally and with the spirit of the world, independent of the Church, outside of the realm of Sacred Tradition, and outside of the pathway which our faith has walked throughout the ages. Let us not try separate, divergent pathways because we do not know to what chaotic confusion and doubt they may lead us. Let us build upon the existing structures of the Church with faith and love, and let us not destroy it with our individualistic, human theories and doubts.

What About the New Ideas of Each Age?

Faith is life and life needs tradition, roots, and history. New ideas in religion come out of the life of the faith; they refer mainly to the meaning and the life experience of the content of faith, the experience of our relationship with God. Any new ideas that may arise can be lived within the one Tradition of faith. We can live any new idea within the Sacred Tradition of the Church; we can enrich the spiritual life of the Church without going outside the definitions and the pathways of the original faith, of the first roots and expressions of the faith. Nothing in the realm of the spiritual things of the faith grows old. They are given by God and do not change in their essence. Only depth and experience is needed. The Holy Spirit is working in the Church from the day of Pentecost. All those who have a greater knowledge and zeal can certainly work harder within the Church; they can use their talents and benefit the Church and attain to the heights that the Saints attained and become friends of Christ and of God the Father. This, after all, is the purpose of the Christian: to live the presence of God within his heart, to deepen his faith, and to rise up even into the third heaven.

F. CONCLUDING QUESTIONS AND REFLECTIONS

The Real Enemy of the Faith

The Christian Faith, in its historical journey, has met with many problems: disbelief, heresy, unbelief, and even persecution. All of these problems were overcome by the steadfastness and unity of the Church in her faith and allegiance to Christ, the Lord, and Savior, as well as by the hope for a better future, for a life in the absolute love of God and of Christ.

The enemy of religion is not atheism, as we often tend to think. Atheism is overcome by the faith of the Church, for there are no true atheists. Everyone believes in something that is eventually deified, or some people will finally deify themselves. It is most instructive to consider Marxism, which fought religion and promised freedom and salvation to the world, but which is now fallen as a philosophy of life. The work of the Church is to take advantage of this situation; to present the Christian faith in its originality, as the true source of real freedom and salvation; to reveal the Christian life as the power of divine love transforming people into a new creation.

Another problem of faith is the idea that man has come to believe that he "has come of age," that he knows everything, including the invisible things of the faith and God Himself. Modern man does not accept anything as traditional and authentic unless he can approve of it with his own mind. "Whatever I don't understand, doesn't exist." Thus he cannot believe in God, in miracles, and becomes indifferent to matters of faith. The measure of all things is the mind, the ego, which seems to reflect "the maniac arrogance of knowledge," as someone expressed it. It is a horrible thought to think that you know everything. Socrates said: "There is one thing that I know and that is that I do not know anything" well enough. St. Paul also reminds us: "If anyone imagines he knows something, he does not yet know as he ought to know" (1 Cor. 8:1-3). If we could just go out a little from earth, from ourselves, we would see that, concerning the world's mysteries, we are still tiny ants running about the little sphere we call earth, as it rotates on its axis and around the sun in the infinite universe. Then, perhaps, as rational beings that we are, we would think more seriously about God, the world, and ourselves. Only Christ, who is outside of the world, can really say what we are. St. Paul who knew himself in Christ says: "It is no longer I who live, but Christ who lives in me" (Gal. 2:20; 6:14-16; 1 Cor. 1:22-24).

The pride of knowledge is the oldest story of humanity. Sacred Scripture presents this as a story from the very beginning in Genesis, chapter 3. Adam wanted to be like God, to know everything. "And they knew that they were naked," says Scripture. The best knowledge for man is to know God. "This is eternal life, that they know thee the only true God and Jesus Christ whom thou have sent" (Jn. 17:3). Faith does not have an argument with rationality, the intelligible expression of the faith, but with rationalism, which is the habit of accepting reason as the supreme authority in matters of belief and spiritual truth.

F. CONCLUDING QUESTIONS AND REFLECTIONS

Another problem, an extension of the previous one, is the lack of hunger and thirst for salvation and for a future life. Christianity is a faith of redemption and salvation. Many people today who do not practice their faith have a spiritual anorexia. They do not hunger for religious and spiritual food. They are not thirsty for the righteousness and the kingdom of God (Mt. 5:6; 6:33). They seek only the present, the concrete and worldly goods of this life. We all know that the present without roots in the past, and without hope for a better future, does not contain the fullness of the meaning of life. It is merely something ephemeral and uncertain. And yet the present life, with its problems and its temporal promises, preoccupies us so much that we do not find time to think or imagine a better future. We become slaves to the temporal that cannot give us something that is steadfast, abiding, and satisfying to our soul. Thus we have no thirst for something higher, divine, or eternal.

Many people today have lost the necessary respect for Christ and God. Others again, who cannot deny the existence of God, imagine God somewhere far away from the world, as Deism teaches. Still, others imagine God to be dead, that is, non-existent in their lives and in the world. All of these things are being said, not by conviction that there is no God acting in the world, but rather with the wish that man may be left more independent and as a god unto himself upon the earth. But man cannot be God; he cannot undertake the responsibility for the world. Man is only a co-worker with God.

What is the Cause of All This?

Is it the fault of the Church, of her leaders, of our theology, of our doctrines? Is it the fault of the oftentimes less than exemplary life of the Christians? Christians are human beings. They do not present themselves always with the same zeal of faith and love. From the time the Church was organized as a force in the world, it has taken on a more or less worldly character. The Church is always in danger of becoming worldly, that is, part of this world. The Lord prayed to the Father not to take us out of the world, but to protect us from the influence of the powers of this world, to remain saints, separated, set apart from this world, dedicated and united with God in Christ if we are to draw the world as a whole to God (Jn. 17:14-23).

Christian nations in general and the Christians who live in nations that are not Christian do not reflect a living spiritual nobility that would make the non-Christians envious and desirous to become themselves Christians. Christ prayed that we all become one flock with one shepherd (Jn. 10:16; Rom. 11:11-14), but sadly this is not yet the case. Even the Church is somehow divided.

This is the reason why many people from the world can say to us today: "You have abandoned the love you had at first" (Rev. 2:4). They may also challenge us with this: "Unless I see... I will not believe" (Jn. 20:25).

F. CONCLUDING QUESTIONS AND REFLECTIONS

7. *Religion, Faith, Mind, and Heart*

Man is by nature a religious being and related to God. Man is indeed created in the image and likeness of God, and needs to be with God, to know God, who is his Archetype. Man also needs to know himself, his origin, his place in the universe, and before God. Man needs to know what is the meaning of his life in the world. God on the other hand is invisible, infinite, and incomprehensible in His essence. God dwells in unapproachable light and no man has ever seen or can see Him (1 Tim. 6:16; Jn. 1:18). Man cannot see God with his physical eyes alone, or understand Him with his mind alone. We know God only by faith and in His divine energies as He providentially acts and cares for the world. "Now faith is the assurance of things hoped for, the conviction of things not seen" (Heb. 11:1; Rom. 1:20).

Faith is a matter of the heart and not of the mind. The radar of the heart can penetrate realms of reality where our mind cannot enter by itself. The heart discerns tons of music and sees spiritual treasures which our eyes cannot see and our ears cannot hear (1 Cor. 2:4-16; 2 Cor. 12:1-10). The heart does not see the world just as a thing to be exploited, but as a transparent reality through which it can perceive the invisible creator. "The heavens are telling the glory of God, and the firmament proclaims his handiwork" (Ps. 19:1). "O Lord, how manifold are thy works! In wisdom has thou made them all." (Ps. 104:24; Gen. 1:1-32). Through the beautiful nature of the created world, God indeed speaks to us about His love and wisdom. We in turn must hear Him and receive His message, and faithfully confess: "I believe in one God the Father, the Almighty, maker of heaven and earth and of all things visible and invisible."

We see God, especially in our heart. We are created in the image of God, and in a pure heart, one can see the image of the invisible God. Our heart is the altar where God meets man and enters into a dialogue with him. God speaks to our heart and our heart answers back to God. The pure in heart can see God, as Jesus assured us. "Blessed are the pure in heart for they shall see God" (Mt. 5:8).

Eyes to See and Ears to Hear

To see God and hear His voice from the universe and to see the glory of God in Christ we must have "ears" to hear and "eyes" to see. We must have an open and receptive heart and the will and love to accept the message of the voice of God in Christ and in the universe. We need to entertain the message of God in our heart; to believe and to come to a personal communion with God. We approach God with our heart, in faith, awe, and worship, rather than with our mind. God is heart and He wants our heart, not our mind. "My son, give me your heart!" (Prov. 23:26). Therefore our Lord divides the people into those who see and those who do not see God in Him and in the universe He created. "For judgment, I came into this world, that

F. CONCLUDING QUESTIONS AND REFLECTIONS

those who do not see (the poor in spirit who thirst for God) may see, and that those who see (the proud who think they know everything) may become blind" (Jn. 9:39). They close their hearts and remain in spiritual darkness. The truth for them remains veiled (2 Cor. 4:2-6).

Everyone to some extent can see God in the miracle of the world and hear His voice in the beauty of our heart, and yet some do not hear and do not see the glory of God in Christ (Jn. 1:14); they cannot believe. They are deaf and blind to the spiritual and divine truth. This unbelief does not come from the conviction that there is no God, for no one can prove the absence of God in the beautiful world. Unbelief or ignorance of the spiritual truth is rather a willing refusal to listen to the whispering of God through the beauty and harmony of the world and through the clear message of salvation through the Person of Christ. People deny the presence of God so that they may be the only god in the world. This is a hybris, a usurpation of the place of God by man, which has started from the very beginning of the first human beings (Gen. 3:4-7; 2 Thess. 2:3-4). Man is indeed created as lord of the world, but under the lordship of God the Creator and Savior of the world (Gen. 1:26-28; Heb. 2:6-8).

Faith is a Demand of the Heart

We are created in the image and likeness of God and we have to live in communion with God. Our heart cannot find its peace unless we find ourselves in God. If our heart does not feel God and does not seek the transcendent kingdom of God, we are spiritually deaf and blind; spiritually dead.

Faith is a Meeting With God

Faith is not the knowledge and the confession of certain religious thoughts. God is not a subject to be studied and to be known by our mind. God is a Person and we, as persons, need to meet Him as a Person and have a personal relationship with Him. We need to speak to Him as "Our Father" and to listen to Him as His children. If we have not reached this level of a conscious personal relationship with our God, the creator, and Father, we are not yet believers. God is a Person and wants our personal father-child relationship.

In Sacred Scripture, the whole history of humanity is a God-man relationship. God first selects certain people. He speaks with them in a person-to-person dialogue, and through them, He leads His people to their ultimate purpose, to become the true kingdom of God (Gen. 3:16; 6:13 ff; 18:17-33; Ex. 33:11; Mt. 28:18-20).

The climax of this God-man relationship we have in the Person of our Lord Jesus Christ. In Christ, God speaks to us in the Person of His Logos-Son. In Christ, we have the last invitation of God to man, an invitation to come and to live in communion with God. Indeed, "God was in Christ reconciling the world to himself" (2 Cor. 5:19-21; Jn. 3:16). For this reconciliation our Lord prayed on the very night of His betrayal, "that they (all the believers) may be one even as we (Father and

F. CONCLUDING QUESTIONS AND REFLECTIONS

Son) are one. I in them and thou in me, that they may become perfectly one" (Jn. 17:20-24). This is the final goal of man and the world, to be one with God.

A Living Faith

Our faith is indeed a God-man personal relationship and this is a matter of life and death. Our faith must have the first place in our life, and not be something secondary or unimportant in our life. We live by faith, by our relationship with God. Therefore our faith must be alive, real, conscious, sincere, and fervent, and not lukewarm and half-hearted (Mt. 17:20; 21:21; Rev. 3:15-16).

God does not impose faith upon us. He invites us to believe and to share His paternal love and glory. We answer with our love; we believe and commit ourselves to God, and with a filial love for Him and in obedience to Him we live our lives in God. "For from him and through him and to him are all things. To him be glory forever. Amen." (Rom. 11:36).

The Christian lives by faith. The whole life of a Christian is a life of unceasing prayer and worship. This worship is not just a recital of our prayers; it is a real personal communion and dialogue with God. It is a life of communion with God in Christ. We thank God for the so many things He gives to us, and especially for His love for us in Jesus Christ (1 Cor. 1:23-26), and we "commit ourselves and one another and our whole life to Christ our God." Thus our whole life and our worship is a eucharist, a thanksgiving to God by all the people of God. We live and do everything in the name of our Lord Jesus Christ and to the glory of God the Father. We live in Christ and Christ lives in us (Rom. 14:7-9; 2 Cor. 5:15; Gal. 2:20). A Christian cannot do or even think of anything which is not of the will of God. "Thy will be done," is his constant prayer (Mt. 26:42; Lk. 1:38; 22:42).

If we do not live our faith as a daily personal communion with God in Christ we are not yet true Christians, united into one Body, the Church, with one Head, our Lord Jesus Christ.

Is the Christian Religion Difficult?

Yes, it is, but all of the good things in life are difficult. "All good things are achieved with great effort." Christian faith wants us to know God and His love in Jesus Christ; to give our heart completely to God and to live our life as images of God in faith and love. However, when one accepts the Christian faith freely as a rule of life, then it becomes easy. The Christian religion in its essence is a personal relationship of man with God. Where God is concerned, everything is possible.

Religion ss a basic element in life and it has served as a foundation for many civilizations. With the light of divine revelation, religion is the main pedagogue of individual persons and of society. If we overlook religion, if we repress our religious emotions into the subconscious, we lose the peace of our soul, and are led to destruction, both as individuals and as societies.

F. CONCLUDING QUESTIONS AND REFLECTIONS

Religion does not hold us back from progressing in life. On the contrary, religion enriches, ennobles, and beautifies our life. Without faith in God and eternity, our life as human beings remains poor, imperfect and does not yet have its full meaning.

The Christian religion in particular gives us the full meaning of life, a life in the present, with our roots in the past, in God, and with an opening of hope for a better future. Our Christian faith gives us our rightful position in the world and before God. The world was made by God for man, and it moves toward perfection with the cooperation of man, and not by his domination (Gen. 2:15; Rom. 8:18-25). The greatness of man is derived from being a coworker with God. We are not masters of the world, but coworkers with God in building the kingdom of God, which has been prepared for us from the beginning of the world (Mt. 25:34). With our faith in Christ, enough light is shed on the mystery of God, man, and life.

St. Irenaeus and St. Athanasios said that God creates and saves the world with His "two hands," the Son and the Holy Spirit. It may be said that we, too, like small children, move within the hands of God. In the duration of our present life we build up our "little houses" and tear them down, and we build them up again until we find ourselves with Him in eternity. All things move toward this goal. This is how St. Paul envisioned this truth, as he meditated on the election and the destiny of Israel. All things come from God; they exist with the help of God and proceed toward God, their final goal. "O the depth of the riches and wisdom and knowledge of God! How unsearchable are his judgments and how inscrutable his ways! 'For who has known the mind of the Lord, or who has been his counselor?' 'Or who has given a gift to him that he might be repaid?' For from him and through him and to him are all things. To him be glory forever. Amen" (Rom. 1:1, 33-36; Col. 1:16-17).

This is the meaning of life according to Christian faith. This is why everyone must know our Christian faith well, and live by it, in all of the depth and height of its teachings. We must uphold it and live it as a religion of living faith, and not as a religion of theory that seeks to satisfy our mind or the temporal requirements of a particular period. Nor should it be a religion of formalities and external practices, or even of a future life only. Our Christian faith must be a real experience of our relationship with God, an authentic life in God here and now with certain hope for an eternity with our Lord Jesus Christ.

We all live our Christian faith together, as a community, not as individuals, but as members of the one Church, the one people of God, the one Body of Christ. There, in the community of faith, as brothers and sisters in God, we help each other and together draw strength and grace from God to continue the struggles of our daily life. All of us are dedicated to our duty, to our Lord and Savior Jesus Christ. Each one contributes with his or her talent, and we live in a competition of faith and love for God and man, ever seeking to build a natural life, a life in God both here and now and with the light of hope to touch eternity.

F. CONCLUDING QUESTIONS AND REFLECTIONS

In our worship, and particularly in the Divine Liturgy, we live together with the angels and the saints and with Christ, and we partake of the heavenly gifts of divine grace. Thus, we experience the kingdom of God upon earth, and we anticipate its fulfillment at the Parousia of the Lord. This is the reason why Christ came into the world: to call us back to God, to the eternal kingdom of God (Jn. 17:21-26; Rev. 22:3-5). Amen.

www.ingramcontent.com/pod-product-compliance
Lightning Source LLC
Chambersburg PA
CBHW031434160426
43195CB00010BB/729